THE
ROAD TAKEN

THE ROAD TAKEN

A Guide to the Roads and Scenery of Mayo

MICHAEL MULLEN

NONSUCH

First published 2008

Nonsuch Publishing
73 Lower Leeson Street
Dublin 2, Ireland

British Library Cataloguing in Publication Data.
A catalogue record for this book is available from the British Library.

ISBN 978 1 84588 577 9

Typesetting and origination by The History Press
Printed in Great Britain

Contents

Introduction:
The ground beneath your feet

The mountains of Mayo are soft of outline. They are smooth-backed, often magnificent and never sharp or irritating. Time, wind, rain, frost and waves, these enemies of soft strata, have worked their power on higher mountains and have left us the hard cores. They are mountains fashioned in volcanic conditions within the earth, and pushed up by gigantic forces. They buckled the flat limestone and red sandstone layers above and eventually the soft skin was worn away. The oldest rocks in the county are a billion and a half years old. The gneiss that forms parts of Erris Head is almost two billion years old. A huge variety of rocks are represented in Mayo, from the Precambrian hard core mountains, down to soft red sandstone and limestone strata.

There are great mountain ranges in Mayo, which give it grandeur. To the south of Clew Bay stands Croagh Patrick with its proud hills; it stands like a great pyramid, perfect in its symmetry. The varying light and weather plays upon it, and sometimes it lies clouded and secretive. Sometimes, under firm light it is blue, passing towards purple. At other times it is varying shades of grey. It is our most famous mountain, and the most sacred. It was sacred even before the arrival of St Patrick.

Across the wide and shallow bay and rising above the northern shore lies the Nephin Beg Range. It is not broken by any high summit but rests securely to the north like a high, protective barrier. This range is formed from hard quartzite. It rises out of a blanket bog, which runs to the western and northern coast of the county. There are many spurs running north from this range. From the air they look like the roots of petrified tree trunks. They have been shorn and shaped by the Ice Age as it moved across this landscape like a many-bladed plough. Innumerable lakes have been gouged out by glacial forces. Some writers describe north Mayo as the most desolate expanse in Ireland, while others have gone there to seek tranquillity. It has also been compared to the Steppes of Russia.

Croagh Patrick at the end of a winter's day.

It is only when one arrives at the northern coast of Mayo that one can look into the layered geology of the county. At the Céide Fields there is a platform from which the visitor can gaze down into the tortured sea at the base of high, layered cliffs. Here one sees the rock base that forms the foundation of the Mayo landscape. At the mouth of Clew Bay stands the great mass of Clare Island. It stands alone, taking what the Atlantic can throw at it. In profile, it looks like the great Sphinx at Gaza. Further onwards lie the Corraun Peninsula and Achill Island. Achill is a formidable landscape of mountains, cliffs, sandy beaches, a remote abandoned village, and changing cloudscape.

To the south lies the mountain of Mweelrea. It is the highest mountain in the west of Ireland. The mountain overlooks Killary Harbour, Ireland's only fjord. It is part of a knotted series of mountains running east to the Sheefrey Hills, Maamtrasna and the Partry Mountains. Little grows on the flanks of the mountains. Hardy sheep graze here, seeking meagre sustenance amongst the crags. The eye never rests, for it is constantly being invited to look at some new wonder, some new crag or crevice not noticed before. This is a tough and sparse landscape.

At the base of these mountains lies the land, upon sandstone, limestone, granite, shale and other soft rock. The land is various and is often set out on drumlins, fashioned by the Ice Age. The islands in Clew Bay, with their buff snouts pointing west, are drowned drumlins, and they run across the country to Antrim. These drumlins form the centre of Mayo. Further east there is deep limestone land, and to the north, blanket bog, which stretches forever. Upon this landscape, man has set up his habitation and left his mark. Megalithic man has left an impressive imprint. Bronze Age man, the Patrician Church, the Vikings, the Normans, the Elizabethans and the Cromwellians have also left easily recognizable traces on the county.

Castlebar

Castlebar is set on in a small valley between drumlins. To the south of Castlebar lie five gentle lakes, each carrying the reflection of Croagh Patrick. This is a unique mountain, reaching majestically and cone-shaped into the sky. It is a sacred symbol set against the skyline. These five lakes are linked, and the furthest in this chain is called Bilberry Lake. Out of Lough Lannagh runs the Castlebar River. It is believed that the course of this river was changed in the nineteenth century and it runs evenly through the town between limestone walls.

Many thousands of years ago, Stone Age and Bronze Age men made their way by boat along the old course of this river and set up habitation on the lakesides and on crannogs. In the nineteenth century, while the lake was being drained, Bronze Age remains were discovered there. Above the final lake lies the fort that gives its name to Blackfort, and upon another hill lies another fort called Rathbawn, or 'white fort', yet more evidence of ancient occupation.

The influence of the Patrician Church was strong in Mayo and upon the graveyard hill and facing the lakes lie the remains of an old foundation. It has almost disappeared but the outline is there, so a monastery and a secular settlement must have stood there. Michael Viney writes of the landscape in these early times in *A Smithsonian Natural History*:

> The picture of the landscape in early historic and medieval times conjures up an early Christian countryside rich in variety, with cattle and sheep grazing through an intimate mix of rough grasses and scrub that resulted from a burst of woodland clearance about the fourth century. It was this herb-rich grassland, with ample browsing on alder, willow, and hazel, that supported a sophisticated dairying economy from the late fifth century. The Quinn clann were the dominant clann in the area.
>
> (Viney, M., *Ireland; A Smithsonian Natural History*. Blackstaff Press: Dublin, 2003.)

The Church of Ireland church, overlooking Castlebar.

Evening sky above Castlebar.

Intimate woodland at Castlebar Lake.

The statue of Manannan MacLir in Castlebar.

The name Castlebar is derived from the 'Castle of Barry', indicating a Norman presence in Mayo. We do not know exactly where the castle was built but it was most likely located on the outcrop of rocks where the military barracks now stand. There is no lasting record of the Barry presence except in the name given to the town, and their coat of arms. The present town was founded at the beginning of the seventeenth century by John Bingham, ancestor of the Earls of Lucan. Richard Bingham, John's brother, was a formidable Elizabethan figure. He was a battle-hardened soldier and a ruthless buccaneer who fought in several tough campaigns on the continent in the service of Elizabeth. Familiar with the rough life of a soldier, he was also a sailor who would be given charge of his own ship. A zealous soldier, he was sent to Ireland by Elizabeth I to help suppress the Desmond Rebellion. He took part in the massacre of Spanish and Italian soldiers at Smerwich in Co. Kerry.

Richard Bingham was a controversial character. He was appointed governor of the Irish province of Connaught in 1584 and by 1586, had been knighted by Lord Deputy Perrot. His two brothers, John and George, were his assistant commissioners. During Richard's time as governor, the people of Connaught rebelled; the MacWilliam Burke clan of Mayo being the chief insurgents. Bingham dealt with the rebels at the Galway assizes, by sentencing seventy to death for disloyalty to the Crown.

Bingham entered the MacWilliam Burke territory and agreed to withdraw his forces only if the rebels were prosecuted. Perrot then granted a three-month protection for the rebels in return for pledges, and decided that the title of the MacWilliam should be abolished. In July, the MacWilliam Burkes fought again, with a greater number of men behind them. Perrot undermined Bingham's authority and forbade him from moving against them. Bingham, however, assembled his army in Ballinrobe and defeated the MacWilliam Burkes. To pay for the cost of the rebellion, Bingham confiscated part of their property, seized their cattle and demanded large fines. It was through this confiscation that Richard's brother John came into the possession of Castle Barry in Castlebar, which had belonged to eighty-year-old Edmund Burke.

When peace was restored, Richard Bingham was called to England to account for his deeds and later returned to Ireland as a marshal of the Queen's army, but died on his arrival on 18 January 1599. His death was welcomed by the Irish and no tears were shed upon his passing, but by then his family had established itself in Mayo and in Castlebar. In October of 1796, Sir Charles Bingham was created Earl of Lucan.

The Lucans have a long association with Castlebar. George Bingham succeeded his father as third Earl of Lucan on 30 June 1839 and was made Lord Lieutenant of Co. Mayo in 1845. The local residents were not fond of him. He continued to rise through the army's ranks and despite being on half pay he was made a colonel in 1841 and a major general in 1851. At the outbreak of the Crimean War he applied for a post and was made commander of the cavalry division. His brother-in-law, the seventh Earl of Cardigan, was one of his subordinates, commanding the Light Brigade; an unfortunate choice as the two men heartily detested each other. The final Lucan was 'Lucky' Lucan who was famous for being a gambler. We shall meet the notorious Richard Bingham later on our journey through Mayo.

One of the events that put Castlebar on the map was the arrival of the French army under General Humbert in 1798, which is sometimes referred to as 'The Year of the French'. The whole incident has been turned into a novel entitled *The Year of the French* by Thomas Flanagan.

Humbert landed at Kilcummen strand, on Killala Bay, with about 1,100 officers and men of the army of the French Republic. He stormed through Mayo, moving with great rapidity. He approached Castlebar through the Windy Gap during a night of heavy rain, lightning and thunder. The army marched along a track through rough land and bog and arrived out of the dawn to the amazement of the British garrison of Castlebar. The force opposing Humbert, under the command of General Lake, numbered about 1,700 and consisted mainly of Irish militia. There was a short battle and the British army, fearing that they were being attacked from several sides, left Castlebar in a hurry. The incident became known as 'The Races of Castlebar'. Several monuments and memorials commemorate the incident.

While in Castlebar, Humbert established a 'Republic of Connaught' and John Moore, from Moorehall outside Castlebar, was elected president. John Moore later died in Waterford as a British prisoner; his remains were taken home and interred on the mall in a triangular piece of earth on which stands a monument to commemorate the event.

Eventually Humbert failed, having stayed in Castlebar for too long. After the defeat at Ballinamuck the Irish rebels where hunted down like vermin and executed. And as for General Humbert, he was shortly repatriated in a prisoner exchange, and later participated in several Caribbean campaigns for Napoleon Bonaparte. He was appointed governor of Saint-Domingue (now Haiti), but as a committed Republican, his displeasure at Napoleon's imperial pretensions led to a fall from favour and exile to Brittany.

Coming under increasing scrutiny and fearful of arrest, Humbert fled to the United States in 1808. He settled in New Orleans, once again fighting the British at the battle of New Orleans in the War of 1812, and briefly participating in the Mexican War of Independence in 1814. He then lived peacefully and taught fencing in New Orleans until his death. All the names of Napoleon's generals are inscribed on the *Arc De Triomphe* except for Humbert's. He had ingratiated himself with Napoleon's sister and the emperor was far from amused. (Stephen Dunford Killala – unpublished material.)

Stand on the green in Castlebar and you will observe part of the history of the town. There is a small church built on the side of the green. It was originally a Wesleyan church and the great John Wesley preached there. It is a simple building without ornament. Out of view stands the military barracks, where Barry Castle once stood. It stands on an outcrop of rock and faces the hills and mountains from which General Humbert emerged. During the 'Troubles' several blocks of the barracks were burned. What is left of it overlooks the former residence of Lord Lucan, which was once a convent school and is now a girls' secondary school. The Lucans could walk from their residence through the mall and enter the Protestant church without being exposed to the stares of the Catholic populace. The fine church stands on a hillock, surrounded by an old graveyard, and has solid and dignified outlines. Inside are monumental brasses and plaques marking the presence of a once-vibrant Protestant community. Beside the Presbyterian church there once stood a hanging tree, which has long since disappeared. Many of the '98 rebels were hanged here during the merciless reprisals. Directly opposite is the Imperial Hotel, once called Daly's Hotel. A plaque on the wall commemorates the formation of the National Land League by Michael Davitt and James Daly.

Further along is a formidable courthouse that is built like the entrance to a Greek temple. Close by is the house where Margaret Burke Sheridan, the internationally famous soprano, was born in 1889. She studied at the Royal Academy of Music in London and made her debut there in 1918 as Mimi in *La Bohème*. She sang in La Scala for the first time in 1920 and was very popular with Italian audiences. Despite repeated requests she never sang in Ireland or in the United States. She retired at the height of her fame and lived at the Shelbourne Hotel in Dublin where she died in 1958.

In 1830, Castlebar had an extensive linen industry. Linen and linen yarn were sold in the hall, which still stands in Linen Hall Street. It was an active town with several other significant industries such as tobacco, snuff, soap and candles 'manufactories'.

The impressive façade of Castlebar Courthouse.

The Burke Sheridan home.

Ernie O'Malley was born in Castlebar in 1898. His family moved to Dublin where he studied medicine. He was a prominent officer in the Irish Republican Army and took part in the 1916 Rebellion. Thereafter, his life was varied and interesting. He fought on the Anti-Treaty side of the Civil War, during which he was hit by twenty-one bullets. After an operation, five remained in his body. He was condemned to death but was given a reprieve when doctors said that he would never walk again. After spending some time in Mountjoy Prison, he travelled all over America. He was both a writer and a broadcaster. He wrote the classic *On Another Man's Wound* in 1936, and a sequel, *The Singing Flame*, which was published in 1978.

Jack Riley, also known as the 'The Man from Snowy River' was born in Castlebar in 1841. When he was thirteen he emigrated to Australia. He worked as a gold-digger and a bushman near the border of New South Wales and Victoria. He became famous as a tracker of wild horses and a mountain rider, and was thought of as a brave and adaptable hero. He provided the inspiration for the poem 'The Man from Snowy River', which was written in 1890 by Banjo Paterson. The poem celebrated the mythology and heroism associated with the bush. Jack Riley was buried at Corryong and over his grave stands the following legend, 'In memory of the many from Snowy River, Jack Riley, buried here 16 July 1914.'

Louis Brennan, the inventor of the dirigible torpedo and the gyroscopic monorail, was also a native of Castlebar, and like Jack Riley he emigrated to Australia with his family. He was born on 28 January 1852 at Main Street, Castlebar to Thomas Brennan, a hardware merchant, and his wife Bridget. His father was a gifted mechanical engineer and constructed the first gasworks system in Castlebar. Louis and his two older brothers, Patrick and Michael, did well at school. Patrick went to Australia in 1856, and accepted a teaching appointment in Melbourne. Michael started work as a journalist with the *Connaught Telegraph*, and soon earned a reputation as a caricaturist. He later attended art schools in Dublin and London, and became an artist of merit. Two of his paintings are in the National Gallery of Ireland: 'A Vine Pergola' and 'Church Interior at Capri'. He died in Algiers in 1871 and was buried there.

Thomas and Bridget Brennan sold their business in Castlebar in 1861 and emigrated with their youngest son, nine-year-old Louis, to Melbourne, Australia. It was here that Louis came up with the idea of a dirigible torpedo in 1874, from observing that if a thread is pulled on a reel, the reel will move away. Brennan spent some years working on his invention, and received a grant of £700 from the Victorian government towards his expenses. He patented the Brennan Torpedo in 1877.

So impressed was the British government by his talents that he was brought to England to supervise the development of these torpedoes, which were to guard the coast of England from naval invasion. He also invented the gyroscopic monorail and helped to develop the helicopter. In January 1932 he was knocked down by a car at Montreux, Switzerland, and he died on 17 January. He was made a Companion of the Order of Bath in 1892.

Canon Ulick Bourke, the famed Gaelic scholar, was born in Linenhall Street, Castlebar on 29 December 1829. He wrote a number of works on Irish grammar and its use. He helped enormously in saving the Irish language. There is a plaque at his birthplace bearing the inscription, 'Sa teach seo do rugadh an t-Athair Uilleog de Burca, Scríobhnóir agus scoláire Gaeilge 1829–1887.'(Canon Ulick Bourke 1829–1887, Gaelic writer and scholar, was born in this house.)

Olivia Knight was born at Rathbawn in Castlebar in 1808. Some years ago the house she was born in was demolished, but on the roadway stands a plaque commemorating her birthplace. She wrote for *The Nation* under the name 'Tomáisín'. In the 1860s she emigrated to Australia and on the voyage met the journalist Hope Connolly, whom later she was to marry. They settled down in Queensland, where she died in 1908.

Matthew Archdeacon was born in this town in around 1800. He was a novelist who became a teacher, and his *Legends of Connaught, Connaught in '98*, and *Everard and the Priest Hunter* were based on local traditions about the Penal days, the United Irishmen's Rebellion, and the Tithe Wars. He died in 1835 in destitution.

William Larminie, poet and folklorist, was born in the town and died in 1900. His *West Irish Folk-Tales and Romances* were based on fieldwork done by native speakers in Donegal, Mayo and Galway.

The *Connaught Telegraph* is the oldest paper in Ireland. It was founded by Frederick Cavendish on St Patrick's Day 1828. He was an outstanding champion of the poor and saw the paper through the horrific famine. The advance of the famine was faithfully recorded in stark weekly reports in the paper. Cavendish was born with the confidence of nobility and his journalism was both fierce and fair. He died in 1856. Thereafter, James Daly, 'the Forgotten Mayo Man', became proprietor of the '*Connaught*' and used it to defend the Land League and the small farmer. After that it passed into the Gillespie family and it has remained with that family ever since.

Linen was once sold here, in what is now the arts centre.

The Great Famine hit Castlebar with ferocity. The scenes in the town during the darkest years were truly horrific and the place became a Charnel house. Every day people died in alleyways, and the road leading to the County Home was choked with the dying and the dead. This famine was to leave a dark cicatrise on the communal memory of the area.

Now we leave Castlebar and pass along the road to Westport. The jailhouse once stood on the left, where the new hospital stands. It had been a formidable yet grim limestone building with 140 cells, day and work rooms and airing yards, in one of which was a treadmill for pumping water. Most public buildings in Castlebar at the time were built of limestone and there were several quarries opened in the area. Beyond that again was the Lunatic

Asylum, as it was called at the time. In 1865, the first portion of St Mary's Hospital was built and officially opened on 23 April (St George's Day), 1866. The whole complex spanned over 200 acres.

Further along the road stands the McDonald house, set in a wide green field. It is a very attractive Georgian building, and beside it lie some outhouses. The road to Westport is situated between small hills, gently rolling towards Clew Bay, sometimes with lakes in between small woods of willow, ash and hazel. Now and then a brown bog appears, marked by surface heather and with black banks with the incised marks of slanes. We are surprised, when we reach the crest of Sheeaun Hill, by the impressive and dominant presence of Croagh Patrick. On a fine day one can see the small church that stands on the summit. At its back lies the pilgrim path, white against grey.

Directly in front lie the many islands of Clew Bay, like a pod of dolphins emerging from the sea, and beyond that stands the stark silhouette of Clare Island, once the home of the mythical sea queen, Grace O'Malley, better known as 'Granuaile'.

Clew Bay and its myriad islands.

Westport

Visitors are always impressed by Westport. It is an ordered sea-port town which James Wyatt planned for Lord Sligo. The gentle Carrowbeg River passes beneath limestone bridges and over small waterfalls. It is tree-lined and in autumn the leaves are carried to the sea past Westport House. Beyond the town lie great mountains with massive quartzite cores and the most impressive mountains in the west of Ireland; Croagh Patrick, the Sheefrey hills, Mweelrea Mountains, the Partry Mountains and, further south, the Twelve Pins of Connemara. To the north-west stand other ranges of mountains stretching to Achill and Erris, as well as the imposing and singular Mount Nephin.

Westport's wealth was drawn from the sea. Great warehouses filled with grain and hides stood beside the quays. They had fallen into decay but have now been restored in a sympathetic fashion and turned into apartments, which has brought vigour and life to the harbour side of the town, and in the summer it now possesses a Parisian gaiety. Westport is the gateway to some of the most spectacular scenery in Ireland.

It was the third Earl of Sligo, or plain John Browne, who undertook the work of improving not only his stately home, but the town itself. He engaged James Wyatt to design Westport. James Wyatt's life was active and interesting and he was the architect of many fine buildings in England. He was born in 1746 and he became active in Westport around 1780. This was an age of elegance, which is still evident in Westport. It has a dignified town centre in the Georgian architectural style, and is one of the few planned towns in the country. The Octagon in Westport is delightfully balanced, and on one side of it stands a Georgian theatre designed by Wyatt. As Thackeray wrote in *The Irish Sketch Book*:

> Nature has done much for this pretty town of Westport; and after nature, the traveller ought to be thankful to Lord Sligo, who has done a great deal too.

The Carrowbeg River in Westport.

Where waters fall at Westport Bridge.

Right: The clock tower in Westport, once called the 'Four-Faced Liar'.

Below: The new married to the old in Westport.

Warehouse development in Westport.

> In the first place, he has established one of the prettiest, comfortable inns in Ireland, in the best part of the little town, stocking cellars with good wines, filling the house with neat furniture, and lending it is said to a landlord gratis, on condition that he should keep the house warm and furnish the larder and entertain the traveller.
>
> (Thackeray, W.M., *The Irish Sketch Book*. Henry Frowde: London, 1845.)

Westport entertained many travellers before the arrival of Thackeray, and continued to do so after his departure. It has always been a town of culture, music and literature. This tradition continues. Many writers and painters have lived here, or lingered for a year or two. In the more recent past Harry Kernoff painted some wonderful pictures of the town that have a strange mid-European quality to them.

Mícheál de Búrca, who was born in 1913 and died in 1985, was a sensitive artist whose themes included scenes from the west coast of Ireland; fishermen drawing up their currachs on beaches, great cloudscapes, seascapes and the ever-present mountains. He is sensitive to the environment in which he was brought up, and it is only now, after his death, that the value of his work is being appreciated.

Eric Cross, a scientist and writer, spent his final years here, living just outside of Westport. He will always be remembered for his book *The Tailor and Ansty*, which was published in 1942. In it, he recorded the life of the tailor Tim Buckley and his wife Ansty.

Owen Hanney was a Protestant clergyman. He wrote under the name 'George A. Birmingham'. He was a Belfast man who came from a Unionist background, but his sympathies were nationalist. He arrived in Westport in 1892 and remained here until 1916. He wrote in order to support his meagre income, and his writing career flourished. His titles run to well over sixty books and he was very popular in his time. His play *General John Regan* created controversy in Westport. It satirised Irish small-town life during the first decade of the twentieth century. The story deals with the consequences of a returning American's practical joke in persuading the townspeople of Ballymoy to erect a statue of an imaginary local hero supposed to have played a part in the liberation of Bolivia. It had a successful run in London but led to riots in Westport. The following report tells the story:

On Wednesday, 4 February , 1914, the performance of George A. Birmingham's *General John Regan*, in Westport, County Mayo, punctuated by catcalls throughout the first act, was stopped during the second act when angry protesters stormed the stage … Chairs were hurled, stage properties and scenery destroyed, the theatre itself badly damaged. The actor playing the Catholic parish priest was the focus of the attack. Rioters ripped off his Roman collar and, after leaving the theatre, burned it in the Octagon [Westport's town centre] … The riot was quelled only after the intervention of the parish priest, Father Canavan, who pleaded for order. Twenty young men described as students were arrested.
(Dean, J.F., 'The Riot in Westport: George A. Birmingham at Home' *New Hibernia Review*, vol. 5, pp. 9-21.)

Owen Hanney died in London in 1950.

John McBride, one of the leaders of the 1916 Rising, was born in Westport in 1869. His career was varied. He studied medicine but later abandoned this pursuit. He joined the Irish Republican Brotherhood, and when the Boer War broke out he left for South Africa. He was commissioned with the rank of Major in the Boer army and given Boer citizenship. After the war he travelled to Paris. In 1903, he married the Irish Nationalist Maud Gonne, whom he had met in 1900 and through whom he met W.B. Yeats. The following year their son Sean McBride (who won the 1974 Nobel Peace Prize) was born.

After the marriage failed, amid accusations of domestic violence, he returned to Dublin. Maud Gonne separated from McBride but never remarried. He joined in the Irish Rising and was executed on 5 May 1916, two days before his fifty-first birthday. Facing the British firing squad, he said, 'I have looked down the muzzles of too many guns in the South African war to fear death and now please carry out your sentence.' He is buried in Arbour Hill Cemetery, Dublin.

At the beginning of the quays lies Cinnamon Wharf. Great warehouses once stood along the quay and above Cinnamon Wharf. These derelict warehouses have been attractively restored and have brought vitality to the quay. If you turn right and pass through the gates of Westport House here, you will see that quiet and calm reign. Beneath an ornamental bridge, water from the Carrowbeg River widens into a man-made lake. The waters fall over a ledge, down towards the sea.

Colonel John Browne (1638-1711), who built the original Westport House, married Grace O'Malley's great-great-granddaughter Maude Burke. He was a Roman Catholic who fought on the Williamite side in the War of the Two Kings. His descendants, however, converted to the established Church of Ireland and prospered. Many Irish families, in order to retain their estates, did the same. The original section of this mansion, the East Front, was built in the 1730s to the design of Richard Castle for John Browne, afterward the first Earl of Altamont. In 1778, three sides were added, probably by Thomas Ivory. These changes distorted the exterior proportions of the building somewhat, but the interior is splendid, owing chiefly to the redecoration by James Wyatt, who was hired by the third earl. Especially attractive, is the large dining room with its fine plasterwork. Family portraits adorn the walls, as do several impressive landscapes by the Irish painter James Arthur O'Connor. In the small dining room is the 'Mayo Legion Flag' brought from France by General Humbert when he landed at Killala Bay in 1798.

On the way to Murrisk the woods are small and close. They are, in a sense, primal woods, with sally, hazel, small oaks and silver birch. The pilgrim pathway to Croagh Patrick begins in Murrisk, beside Owen Campbell's pub. Across the road stands the stark, ghostlike famine ship created by John Behan. It serves as a reminder of the suffering of local people during the dreadful years of the famine; the hunger, the coffin ships, and the flight from a blighted land.

The eye now turns to the sacred mountain called Croagh Patrick. It was sacred for many thousands of years before St Patrick climbed 'the Reek'.

There he prayed, banged against heaven's gate and extorted extravagant promises from God Himself. It had been visited by pagan pilgrims, and the outline of their habitations can be seen upon the Reek. The great pilgrimage to the Reek takes place on Garland Sunday. The pilgrims, some carrying pilgrims' staves, others barefoot, make their way to the blessed summit. A chain of humanity is linked together as the pilgrims make their way to the top and others descend. There at the top, at the small chapel, they move around in a massive prayer wheel, chanting out the rosary and knocking at heaven's door, as St Patrick did. At the summit of this sacred mountain they wait for the dawn. There is a false dawn, and a grey dawn, followed by a silver dawn, and then the wide landscape beneath and beyond is revealed. The islands, with sleek backs and snouts pointing west, seem to awaken from a nocturnal sleep. Beyond the bay lie the Nephin Beg Range, Corraun Peninsula and, further away, Achill Island. To the south stand the firm shapes of Mweelrea, the Sheefrey Hills, and the Partry Mountains, whose sides have been sheared and rutted by the melting ice cap. Once, their lonely and brooding peaks stood above the plains of even ice.

The misty presence of Croagh Patrick.

At the foot of Croagh Patrick.

By the seashore lie the ruins of Murrisk Abbey. The abbey was set close to the sea in a most pleasant place, in quiet surroundings. A gentle mountain stream runs across sand pebbles and enters the sea. Ash and rowan trees grow about the ruins. Murrisk Abbey was once a most favoured place; Grace O'Malley attended church here.

In 1456 Hugh O'Malley, an Augustine friar from Banada in Co. Sligo established the monastery in Murrisk. It was suppressed during the Reformation but managed to survive in a twilight world. There is a silver chalice now in Ballintubber Abbey bearing the following inscription, 'Pray for the soul of Theobald, Viscount Mayo and his wife Maeve ne Chonchonre, who had me made for the monastery of Murske in the year of our Lord 1635.' Then there is Father William Bourke's beautiful poem, written in Irish in 1730. He laments his transfer inland:

My holy vow of obedience
Bids me remain here.
And abandon lovely Murrisk
And the music of the Sea.
(Mullen, M., *Mayo, The Waters and the Wild*. Cottage Publications: Down, 2004.)

Perhaps the most interesting and troubled friar to be associated with Croagh Patrick, however, is Friar Cassidy, or '*An Caisideach Bán*'. The influence of his greatest poem spread through Irish culture in the dark eighteenth century. He was a highly emotional man, desiring women when within the monastery, desiring to return to a chaste life when he was outside it. Cassidy was ordained an Augustinian friar in the late eighteenth century, but was soon thereafter defrocked on account of his marriage to a young woman. He left for France, joined the army, deserted and went to Hamburg, and returned to Ireland as a wandering seanchaí. Murrisk Abbey is now a quiet and sacred spot and sleeps beside the sea, all tempests now past.

Louisburgh

This town is situated close to the southern coast of Clew Bay. To the east and rising gently, are twin hills carrying woods on their slopes. To the west the land lies open, a patchwork of field and bog running towards the Sheefrey Hills. Once, the traveller H.V. Morton wrote about Connemara, 'I know where the world ends'. The European world ends here and its final border runs from Donegal, through Louisburgh, and down to the sharp tip of Kerry.

Louisburgh is a planned town, and was built in 1795 by the Marquis of Sligo. It is planned in a tidy fashion and the centre is octagonal, with four roads and four façades. Before he built the town there was a Christian presence here. There has always been a Patrician presence in such places as Aran, Boffin, Cahir Island and Innismurray, which suggests that Patrick belonged more to Connaught than to Ulster.

Officially the town was founded by Lord Altamont, in the patent given to him in 1796. Thus, on certain days the small farmers and others could sell their produce at Louisburgh and the Earl of Altamont could gather his taxes. The Altamonts were always conscious of land and of the organization of their properties, which stretched from Clew Bay to the Killaries. Much of the land is lonesome and remote.

By 1798 the town had become well developed. Many of the tenants came from Northern Ireland and were flax growers and linen weavers. Thousands fled to Mayo after persecution in 1795; it is said that 4,000 Catholics fled to Mayo after the 'Battle of the Diamond', as we have already seen. At the official foundation of Louisburgh these weavers and flax growers were amongst the first inhabitants. It was a huge migration. They carried with them their trades, and they were diligent people. They rejuvenated the linen trade, which then flourished for several years. Thirty families settled in Louisburg in 1796. Protestant and Catholics lived side by side in this new town.

The Octagon in Louisburgh.

Reverend Robert Potter, who was curate during the grim era of the famine, made a plea for help during the darkest days of this great hunger and died of famine fever. This famine fever was the most widespread and deadly of the diseases that we associate with the famine. It consisted of two separate diseases, Typhus and relapsing fever. Both were spread by the common louse and in the crowded and filthy conditions prevailing in homes, workhouses and hospitals, they spread like wildfire among a people whose resistance was greatly diminished by famine.

As was mentioned earlier, the Patrician Church was long established here. Kilgeever church, and churches at Dooghmore and Gowlaown, are remnants of the beginnings of this long tradition. Many stones inscribed with crosses can be found in the area. There was a Catholic church in the area before the town was built. The present church was built in 1862 and dedicated by the powerful and leonine figure of Archbishop McHale. Archbishop McHale, next to O'Connell, exercised a more prolonged influence on the Roman Catholic population of his country than any Irishman of his time. Appointed professor of dogmatic theology at Maynooth, he wrote a series of letters chiefly concerned with controversial questions and Catholic emancipation under the pseudonym 'Hierophilus'. His letters showed great vigour of style and this, coupled with the energy of his character and his eloquence, gained for him from O'Connell the title, 'the Lion of the fold of Judah'. Appointed archbishop of Tuam, he continued his controversial letters. He was a renowned Irish scholar and translated sixty of Moore's melodies into the Irish language, along with six books of *The Iliad* and several portions of the Bible.

But Louisburgh also has a lighter side. According to James Berry in his *Tales of Old Ireland*, there were frequent social gatherings in this area up to the year of the Great Famine of 1846 and he added that, 'the pipes in these days were as plentiful as blackberries in autumn'.

He remembers the last social gathering held on St Patrick's Day before the Famine; the piper, a young man, sat on a chair in the open air, playing 'Haste to the Wedding'. This was Martin Moran, an imposing man who was six foot four tall, who was also blind, and the son of a local farmer. He was considered to be the best player in Connaught in his day.

We leave Louisburgh, and at the end of the town we have three choices. On the one hand we can take the road to Roonah Peer and sail either for Clare Island or Inishturk. On rare days you can take a boat to the blessed island of Caher. During the Irish golden age, the islands of the area were peopled with monks. They sailed these seas easily, and for these hardy mariners Iona and the sacred island of Lindisfarne were never far away. St Brendan would have called to the small monasteries that lay on his route to the Shetlands. But for the moment let us take the road which leads through Killeen and Thallabawn down to the Doovilra. There, upon a wide and white strand, the world of Mayo truly ends. This bay is spotted with small islands and sinister rocks. Standing above this partially-hidden Ireland, stand the Mweelrea Mountains with their high and tough core.

Mweelrea Mountain is the highest mountain in Connaught and is guarded on all sides by craggy slopes giving the impression that it is unconquerable. It is flanked on one side by Killary Harbour, Ireland's only true fjord, and on the other side by Doolough Pass, a glaciated valley. There are no easy ascents of this mighty mountain, and it needs to be approached with care. Reserve a clear day for the climb and enjoy the panorama of the mountains, coast and surrounding islands.

The writers Michael and Ethna Viney live at Thallabawn close to this formidable mountain. Michael Viney has celebrated this area in the same fashion as Thoreau celebrated Walden Pond. He has described this landscape in all its weathers, in all its moods. His writing is lyrical and sensuous and the area has provided him with endless material for his Saturday column in the *Irish Times* and the books which have been inspired by this piece of earth. In his book *A Year's Turning* he writes of the monthly changes in the landscape and its effects upon his life. He looks upon the landscape with loving eyes. He has done more than most to direct our attention to our landscape and its varied beauty, and to point out the necessity of preserving what we possess before we spoil it:

> The first touch of sun these mornings, spilling out of Killary like gold from a crucible, lights up the unfenced commonage along the shore: first, the rough creggans and ivied cliffs beyond the lake, then the great flat lawn of machair behind the dunes. It is all very wild and primal looking, especially if the swans are flying. As the sun gets up over Mweelrea and rakes the amphitheatre of the hillside, it discovers bright green lozenges of land where boulders have been swept aside and the land reseeded, but also fields where nothing much has changed in a hundred years.
> (Viney, M., *A Year's Turning*. Blackstaff Press: Belfast, 1996.)

Clare Island

From Roonagh Quay you take the boat to Clare Island, which stands like a sentinel at the mouth of Clew Bay. It deserves a book to itself, and indeed it has such a book, for the great naturalist Robert Lloyd Praeger visited this island with a team of naturalists and conducted a unique and thorough survey. Anne Chambers wrote a comprehensive life of the Elizabethan sea queen Grace O'Malley, while Eleanor Fairburn wrote the magnificent novel *The White Sea Horse* on the same subject. Several works of fiction have been written about the legendary figure of Grace O'Malley. She lived through a piratical age and was a contemporary of Queen Elizabeth. Their lives had a number of similarities. Grace belonged to a race of seafarers who knew the sea in all its moods and knew all the sea lanes. The O'Malleys possessed fine ships and carried out commerce with France and Spain. Grace married twice; her first husband was an O'Flaherty and by him she had three children. She had one son by her second husband 'Iron' Dick Burke. Her second husband would later succeed her, and he became known as 'Tibbet of the Ships'. She was thus married into the Gaelic stock of Connaught. She was powerful enough to offer Sir Henry Sidney three galleys and two hundred men.

Her life was tempestuous, like that of Elizabeth and all the buccaneers of the age. In the late sixteenth century, she could not keep the advance of English power and law at bay. In 1593, when her sons Tibbot Burke and Murrough O'Flaherty, and her half-brother Donal-na-Piopa, were taken captive by the English governor of Connaught, Sir Richard Bingham, Grace sailed to England to petition Elizabeth I of England for their release. Elizabeth apparently took to Grace, who was three years older, and the two women reached sufficient agreement for Elizabeth to grant Grace's requests, provided Grace's support for many Irish rebellions and her piracy against Great Britain ended. Their discussion was conducted in Latin, as Grace spoke

Clare Island in the distance.

no English and Elizabeth spoke no Irish. But the visit did not tame Grace or her warlike ways. She died a sad old woman, perhaps at Rockfleet Castle, in 1603. Elizabeth died in the same year.

Between 1909 and 1911 the Belfast naturalist Robert Lloyd Praeger led an exhaustive biological survey of the island, which was unprecedented at the time and served as a template for future studies. Here is what he wrote concerning the island in his classic *The Way I Went*:

Clare Island, anciently Cliara, which I have just mentioned, is a fascinating place. My first experience of it began weirdly. Noting that its botany was curiously unknown, my wife and I crossed over from Roonah Quay in the post-boat on the evening of July 1903. It was dead calm, with an oily roll coming in from the west. All the hills around were smothered in a white mist, which over the island formed an enormous arch, solid enough seemingly to walk on, and descending nearly to sea level. We lurched across in an ominous stillness, and darkness descended before it was due, as we groped our way to the little quay. Next morning, when we wished to get away to explore the island, all was dense mist and heavy rain, still without wind, and all day we fretted in our little cottage, unable to move. Late in the day the rain ceased, and a strange red glow, coming from the north-west, spread through the thinning fog. We hurried out to the north point of the island, and there, just sinking into the ocean, was a blood-red sun, lighting up dense inky clouds which brooded low over the black jagged teeth of Achill Head, rising from a black sea tinged with crimson. It was a scene fitted for Dante's *Inferno*, and if a flight of demons or of angels had passed across in that strange atmosphere it would have seemed appropriate, and no cause for wonder.

(Praeger, R.L., *The Way That I Went*. The Collins Press: Cork, 1947.)

This led to a vast survey of the island. Specialists arrived from Ireland and Europe and built up a very comprehensive picture. While the flora and the fauna were the chief concern, the history and archaeology of the island was studied, as well as place names and family names, native designations of animals and plants, climatology, geology and agriculture.

As you approach the small harbour lying sheltered on the eastern side of the island you note the half-castle, half-tower house of Grace O'Malley looking grimly down on the harbour. The small Cistercian Abbey near the south coast of the island was founded by the O'Malleys and contains the O'Malley Tomb, a possible burial site of Grace O'Malley. The abbey is known for its rare medieval roof paintings. In 1588, a ship from the Spanish Armada was wrecked on Clare Island and its men killed by the O'Malleys. Grace O'Malley lived in a harsh age when the old Irish world was falling apart and she strove hard to survive during tempestuous times.

To the south-west lies the small island of Inishturk. Inishturk means 'wild boar island' and it is rarely visited by tourists. Consequently, its rugged beauty has not been destroyed. The landscape is tough and so the inhabitants relied on the sea to provide them with a living. The British built a Martello tower on the western coast during the Napoleonic Wars.

Even today Clare Island possesses the qualities described by Praeger. The accommodation is much better now and life is comfortable, but the island still possesses rugged charm.

There are many sacred islands off the western coast, for there was a strong monastic presence on all the islands, but there is no island more sacred than Caher Island. The pilgrimage to the Reek ended on this blessed place. When

Doolough: a sad and mysterious lake.

fishermen pass the island they lower their sails in respect, and it is sometimes known as 'the island of the saints'. The carved crosses are of exceptional beauty and simplicity and predate the more ornate high crosses of the eighth century.

We return to the crossroads just outside Louisburgh and move towards Doolough Pass with its dark, menacing beauty.

Towards Leenaun

The road runs evenly along the lake down to Delphi and beyond that to Leenaun in Co. Galway. It is a black lake and one should not linger too long there, for the sadness of the place enters the soul. For the tourist, looking down upon the narrow sheet of water, with the mountains rising sharply on either side, it is breathtaking in its beauty and majestic in its setting. The light plays unevenly with this landscape. Sometimes it is foreshortened by mist, with shapes emerging and withdrawing as the mist swirls or thins. Sometimes the rain falls heavily on the place, turning the exposed rock blue and black. At other times the outline of the mountains is sharp and firm.

It is bare and bleak and possesses an elemental beauty. On the sides of the mountains, barely discernible sheep crop grass amidst the heather. The geology of the area is turned and twisted and beneath it all are pre-Cambrian rocks. The soil is sparse and begrudging. Further on towards Leenaun are black bog, dark streams and Paul Henry-style stacks of turf. For a summer painter, it's a glorious place, with its changing lights, its unspinnable bog cotton, and its billowing clouds, which move across the skies like some strange caravanserai. To those who wish to escape for some weeks to a charming cottage, or a Toblerone-shaped house, it is truly paradise, but to those who work there it is a different matter, for it demands a hard and sometimes lonely life. The Valley of Doolough, with its high mountains and narrow lakes, is filled with sad voices for those who know part of its history – certain historic events stain landscapes and this landscape has been stained by a tragic event.

Lord Sligo looked at a spit of land in the Valley of Doolough and it reminded him of Greece, and so he called the lodge he built there 'Delphi Lodge'. The summer sun must have been shining that day, for the place would never have reminded him of Greece on a wet and windy day.

The famine hit Louisburgh with ferocity. In March of 1847, the potato having failed, 600 starving people made their way to Delphi Lodge in order to apply to the Board of Guardians for food. By the time they got to Louisburgh, many had already perished. The rest had to cross the Glankeen River, which was in full flood, in order to reach Delphi Lodge. Wet and cold, they reached the hunting lodge and while the guardians continued with their dinner they sat on the ground and waited. When they were refused relief or tickets for food, they began the return journey to Louisburgh. It was a bitterly cold night and when they reached a high place called Stroppabue, the wind was blowing so hard that many were blown off the cliff and fell to their deaths in the lake beneath. A simple stone cross recalls the tragic event. This dark moment in history is commemorated each year with the Famine Walk.

However, to the eye uninformed by these events it is a steep, rugged and beautiful spot. The slopes of the mountains run abruptly up from the Doolough, the Mweelrea Mountains and the Sheefrey Hills, pressing in upon the landscape and funnelling the vision down through the valley. There are few places in Ireland with such intense and remote beauty.

Beyond the lake and at the edge of a small lake called Fin Lake, which might be translated as 'bright lake', lies Delphi Lodge. Peter Mandel purchased Delphi Lodge some years ago and it is now one of the finest fishing retreats in Ireland. In his superb book *A Man May Fish*, T.C. Kingsmill Moore celebrated Delphi Lodge and its tenant Alec Wallace:

> Delphi Lodge was a big, rambling house, built around three sides of a square, rather dilapidated, not very comfortable or well furnished, insufficient in bathrooms. Not one of these things mattered for the old house inhaled kindness and welcome. The regular frequenters were a mixed grill, a couple of civil servants from Northern Ireland, some businessmen and the whole gamut of the professions. Despite many points of possible friction I never heard a snarl or a spit. Whether it was the influence of Alec or the house I know not, but everybody was on good terms with everybody else and friendships were formed which lasted till death. That is, maybe a slight exaggeration. There was the very odd pebble – two young guards officers who tried to throw around their very inconsiderable weight and a woman whose aggressive self-assurance was only matched by her ignorance – but these were swallows of only one season and when they applied for future bookings Alec was always unaccountably full up. (Kingsmill Moore, T.C., *A Man May Fish*. Colin Smythe Ltd: Buckinghamshire, 1960.)

Further on and to the left lies Delphi Adventure Centre. It blends in well with the landscape. The dark, brown stone façade suits the buildings. It uses the landscape and the mountains well and is open in all weathers. It tests people against bog, water, and mountain and against themselves. For those locked in the artificial confines of cities and offices, this foundation gives them access to a landscape of grandeur and to pristine beauty and primal remoteness. It is without the mark of urban civilization or the comfort of a controlled landscape.

It is a long and lonely road from Louisburgh to Leenaun. There are very few places in Ireland to compare with this area and the intense delight it engenders. Having escaped the dense pressure of Doolough Pass, the mind is less burdened.

Suddenly you come out of this area and lying below the fern banks is Killary Harbour. Tucked into the base of the mountains lies Leenaun and above it rise the eternal Twelve Bens, or Pins, of Connemara, which are geologically very old, like all the mountains in the area. These mountains are set in Galway, for we are now on the southern borders of Mayo.

Leenaun, situated at the head of Killary Harbour, is often aptly described as the 'gateway to Connemara'. The roads from Maum, Clifden and Westport meet at this point. Killary Harbour extends ten miles inland and, with the mountains rising steeply on either side, provides what is probably the best scenery in Ireland. Walkers have access to Mweelrea, Sheefrey, Partry and Maumturk Mountains. To the naturalist this is a landscape of vital importance.

Blanket peat extends into the upland areas of the Sheefrey Hills and Mweelrea Mountains, where much of the vegetation is heath and acid grassland. Higher up there are cliffs, scree slopes, corrie walls, shales and slates. It is a tough, spare and sparse landscape.

Leenaun is a haven for geologists, naturalists and fishermen. There is good fishing in the local Erriff and Delphi rivers. Well-known beauty spots include Ashley Falls and Doolough Valley, scene of the tragic famine walk. A film adaptation of John B. Keane's play *The Field*, directed by Jim Sheridan, was made in Leenaun in 1989. As you journey towards Leenaun you will hear the sound of Ashley Falls. It is fed by the rains which frequently fall upon the mountains and uplands. In summertime its nature is quiet and placid. It is beautiful in all its moods. One of the most dramatic scenes in the film *The Field* takes place here, when Tom Berenger and Richard Harris confront one another over the primitive question of land. The land may be bleak in Co. Mayo but every rock, bog, bush, and drain can be accounted for and belongs to someone.

Left: A wintery landscape close to Delphi Lodge.

Below: Ashley Falls, where the final dramatic scene of *The Field*, takes place.

We turn left at the signpost which directs us towards Westport. Bearing down upon us are the Partry Mountains, tall, bleak and precipitous. On wet days you notice the small wisps of waterfalls blown this way which, like a girl's flaxen hair, at other times fall directly towards the Erriff River. Sometimes a bare patch of rock breaks through the shallow surface of the flanks and they look like mange on the hide of a healthy animal.

The Erriff River runs pleasantly by the roadside. The Erriff System is comprised of the Erriff River and the two small loughs of Tawnyard and Derrintin. They lie high in the mountains and are best viewed from the top of an enchanted valley above the Sheefrey Woods. The Erriff is one of the premier salmon fishing rivers in Ireland. A spate river, it is characterised by lively streams and deep fish-holding pools.

There is a run of spring fish into the river during the months of April and May, grilse or summer salmon appear in June and the runs continue throughout July, August and the early part of September. Sea trout runs are from early July onwards.

Tawnyard Lough is 250 acres in size and was once the best sea trout lake in the district. The lough is situated high in the hills. To find this magnificent scenery one has to take the road at the end of Doolough and travel towards Liscarney. On the high hills and at a natural platform, you can look down upon Tawnyard Lake with its private islands and its private beauty. Beside the Erriff River stands a wood of sessile oak. The trees are the remnants of our native forests, which once dominated the country. Growing between them are dainty fern and close by the salmon river, with its pebbled pools and sand banks, moves down to the sea. We move towards Westport but we will take a detour to Aghagower. This indeed is a sacred foundation and has been for a long time.

Aghagower

St Patrick was an intrepid traveller. He did not move about as a lonely wanderer. He travelled with an impressive retinue, if we are to believe the descriptions we have in *The Tripartite Life of St Patrick*, written by a north Mayo writer, Tírechán. St Patrick brought with him a household of professionals: a bishop, a priest, a judge, a psalmist, a chamberlain, a bell-ringer, a cook, a brewer, a sacristan, a charioteer, a woodman, a cowherd, three smiths, his carpenters, three embroiderers, three masons and many others.

For over a thousand years, Aghagower had religious control over the baronies of Burrishoole, Murrisk and the many islands of Clew Bay. The saint we associate with Aghagower is St Senach. It is said that when St Patrick arrived at the Field of the Spring he was well received. He was given the grant of lands and he placed his new foundation under Senach, a married man. St Patrick prepared Senach's son Oengus for the priesthood and wrote a catechism for him. Again, we have the practical organiser at work. From here he set out to climb the Reek. It was sacred to the pagans and Patrick wished to leave the Christian mark upon it. The path used today by pilgrims was most likely the same path used by pagan processions on their way from Cruachan in Roscommon. Like Moses, St Patrick would have spent an impressive amount of time on the summit and close to the summit, and then he returned after Lent to Aghagower.

Aghagower translates from Irish as 'the plain of the springs'. One of the monuments still in existence is the 'Leaba Phádraig' (St Patrick's Bed), where the saint is reputed to have slept. Pilgrims performed stations between the bed and the holy well, Tobair na nDeachan (the well of the deacons), which has now dried up.

This charming historic village is dominated by a striking tenth-century round tower and a medieval church, both partly restored. There are many round towers in Mayo and there is always a discussion as to whether they were built for people to take refuge from the Vikings or to direct pilgrims towards a monastery at night. A fire or lantern would burn in the upper storey in order to direct the pilgrims to a place of sanctuary. This round tower was built between 973 and 1013 and legend has it, the top section, having been struck by lightning, landed on the hill of Tavenish, half a mile away.

Within the walls of the monastery lie flat tombstones marking the graves of those buried there. It was believed that if one was buried in such a sacred place, one would pass through the gates of heaven quickly.

We return to Westport through Knappagh. It is a wooded valley and close to Brackloon woods, where oak and birch forests grow. There was, at one point, a church in Knappagh but it is now deconsecrated, as are many other Protestant churches in Mayo. In the old graveyard the author and inventor Eric Cross lies buried. Robert Frost would have loved Brackloon and Brackloon woods.

Though much disturbed, Brackloon represents one of the few good examples of Atlantic, semi-natural oak woodland remaining in Ireland. Due to variations in landscape and soil, the ecosystem supports sessile oak, ash hazel, birch, elm, mountain ash, holly and willow.

Historical accounts suggest that extensive woodland existed in this region prior to 1600. After 1600, population pressure and the use of charcoal for iron smelting combined to reduce woodland regionally, and at Brackloon there is considerable evidence of tree felling and charcoaling:

When John Browne came to inherit his estate in 1635 he would have found Brackloon Oak Wood in pristine condition – mature oak trees, young saplings, Holly, Hazel and Rowan as well as low plants including rare fern, orchid, wood sorrel and others. The Owenwee River added a grace and beauty of the scene and formed a protective boundary on one side.
(O'Reilly, C., *The House in The Wood*. Brackloon National School 1849-1999.)

Castlebar to Mulranny and on to Achill

During the summer, days seem endless in Achill. It is a magical island set in a tempestuous sea. We take the road to Cornanool. On the way you will pass Mallard Lake and beyond that a farm gateway. The pillars are made from two cannon guns. We stop at Brownes of Rehins where the Brownes once lived. The house at the end of the avenue is now dilapidated. Many years ago the lead and the slate roof were sold and thus it fell into decay. H.J.H Browne occupied it when Samuel Lewis's *Topographical Dictionary of Mayo* was published in 1837, about nine years before the famine.

Standing by the side of the grassy and mossy avenue, is a tall and narrow plinth erected by Dodwell Browne, in memory of his wife, who fell from her horse at this spot and was killed. A wood climbs the hill beside the old avenue and here the Brownes are buried.

It is maintained in local folklore that the French established one of their camps close to this house, and it is also believed that Humbert dined here during his time in Castlebar, as guest of the then-owner, Maria O'Donnell Browne. Tradition also has it that Maria gave Humbert a gift of a shirt, while he in turn presented her with a horse, which he claimed had saved his life during the battle of Castlebar.

One now passes on towards Newport. To the right a road runs down past Glenisland to Beltra Lake. The road is marked by long stretches of bog. Here there is old bog oak, exposed by bog cuttings. These ancient tree stumps bleach in the bog trenches and bog pools, lonely, bleak and abandoned. The heathers give the landscape a brown and purple quality. Here and there upon a drumlin hill a farmstead sits, like an island in a buff sea. The whole area is a network of roads where a stranger might stray forever.

Nearing Newport one halts at the Leg of Mutton Lake. It was during the 1961 state visit to Ireland that the Prince and Princess of Monaco visited the two-roomed cottage overlooking the Leg of Mutton Lake at Drimurla where the Princess's grandfather John Kelly had been born in 1857, a few years after the Great Famine. He later emigrated to America.

Newport is one of the most delightful towns in Mayo. The Newport River runs darkly beside the road. It is overhung by trees and in autumn the leaves fall on to the surface and are gently carried away. The river makes its way quietly towards the sea, falling over slight waterfalls. Newport is a comfortable town and the gateway both to Achill and Belmullet. The first thing one notices is the high and arched viaduct spanning the river. It is slender, delicate and constructed from red sandstone. Thomas Wynne, the great Mayo photographer of the 1890s, was at hand to capture its construction. While most railways at the time were built of iron, this was built of stone. Great timber-framed structures support the semi-circular archways and a small crane on a timber platform rides on struts above the structure. The heyday of the railways was coming to an end and this railway, which would eventually lead to Achill, had a short and tragic career.

In 1837, the town, sometimes called Newport Pratt, consisted of one principal street and several side streets, and contained about 230 houses, some of which were well built and of neat appearance. The bridges divide the town in two. On the southern side the houses, with coloured façades, are built tight in beneath a hill; the northern part of the town, with some tall and impressive buildings, runs up a slight incline. The street is broad enough to be called a square, and at the northern end the cars are funnelled into the road which leads to Mulranny.

There is a legend that Columcille was lent a psalter by St Finnian from which he made a copy. This became to be known as *An Cathach*. There followed a dispute regarding the ownership of the copy. The King of Tara attempted to resolve this dispute in a very early copyright ruling and said, 'to every cow her calf, so to every book its copy'. His attempt to resolve the issue failed, however, and the psalter of St Columba passed into the hands of the O'Donnells after the battle of Cul Dremhne in AD 561. St Columba went to Iona in AD 563. It is certain that the manuscript dates from the late sixth or early seventh century, but modern historical scholarship has cast doubts on St Columba's authorship. There is a story connected with this psalter, the first of our manuscripts.

When the old Gaelic system collapsed, the Ramelton branch of the O'Donnells took the guardianship of the *Cathach* upon themselves. After the Treaty of Limerick, Brig. Daniel O'Donnell brought it with him to the

The viaduct with many arches in Newport.

Newport House.

continent. He had a silver case made for it in 1723, as it had suffered much throughout the years and was not in very good condition. Later, he had it placed in a monastery at Louvain, stipulating certain conditions for its retrieval.

More than three quarters of a century were to pass before the *Cathach* came to life again. Upon its discovery on the continent, Sir Neal O'Donnell of Newport had a false pedigree drawn up by the Deputy King of Arms for a fee of £1,000, declaring him head of Clann Dálaigh. With this document he claimed the *Cathach*. His claim was successful and the sacred relic soon found a new resting place in Newport House, Co. Mayo.

But while Sir Neal held the relic, he was not aware of its contents. He believed it to be the repository of bones. It was not until after his death in 1811, when it was formally opened by Sir William Betham, that it was discovered to house a manuscript. This precious manuscript is now in Dublin and is one of the nation's most treasured possessions.

Newport has always been a patriotic town down through the centuries. Fr Manus Sweeney was ordained in the Irish College in Paris in about 1787 and returned to Ireland. When Humbert arrived Sweeney acted as interpreter for the French Captain, Boudet. After the failure of the French invasion he went on the run. He was captured and brought to Castlebar, where he was condemned to death. He was transported to Newport and hanged publicly. He is buried in Burrishoole Abbey.

Major General Michael Kilroy, who belonged to the old IRA, played a leading part in the War of Independence. He was a blacksmith by trade. After a defeat at the Kilmeena ambush he got his column away without loss of life. The ambush at Carrowkennedy was a much greater success, as a large quantity of arms was seized. There was only one photograph taken of his flying column and it became famous thereafter.

There are three churches in Newport. The Protestant church has been deconsecrated. High on a hill over Newport stands St Patrick's church. It is built from red sandstone and is Roman in style, unlike the many Gothic churches in Mayo. The church is made more beautiful with its luminous and deeply-coloured windows by Harry Clarke.

Ernie O'Malley lived close to Newport for many years. He suffered a heart attack in 1953, and died in March 1957, aged fifty-nine. His life as a soldier, tactician, intellectual, critic and traveller has something of an epic character to it. He was the author of a classic entitled *On Another Man's Wounds*. He died at Howth.

In the autumn of 1938 Ernie and Helen O'Malley, after searching for a suitable family home, moved into Burrishoole Lodge. The lodge was an eight-bedroom stone house situated across an inlet from Burrishoole Abbey, the fifteenth-century Dominican priory. Ernie O'Malley was particularly pleased with the purchase, for the location had links to the Clann O'Malley and his ancestor Grace O'Malley. The lodge, with its views of Clew Bay and Croagh Patrick in the distance, appealed to his American wife Helen (*née* Hooker). It also appealed to Ernie's artistic instincts, and Helen extended the building to include a studio for her sculpture. The O'Malleys purchased the buildings and forty acres of attached land in 1941. The property was extended with the purchase of a further thirty acres of land in 1942.

O'Malley met Helen Hooker in the 1930s in America. They married and had three children. They divided their time between Dublin and Burrishoole in Mayo. Hooker and O'Malley devoted themselves to the arts; she was involved in sculpture and theatre, while he made his living as a writer. Eventually, their relationship soured and ended in divorce.

From his spit of land Ernie O'Malley could see Clew Bay and the islands that he loved, and the famous abbey of Burrishoole.

The abbey is situated at the edge of a quiet tidal estuary. The nave, chancel, tower and south transept remain, and there are ruins of domestic buildings and a cloister to the north.

Richard de Burgo, the MacWilliam *Íochtair*, founded the abbey of Burrishoole in 1469 as a friary for the Dominican order. Following his resignation as chieftain of the De Burgo clan, Richard retired to the abbey and died there in 1473. Richard's grandson Tomas 'Crosach' (the scarred) Bourke was responsible for the manufacture of the O'Malley–Burgo chalice for the Burrishoole friars. Tomas was married to Grania O'Malley and both their names, together with the date 1494, are inscribed on the base. This Grania was a great-grandaunt of Granuaile.

In 1652, the abbey was attacked and plundered by Cromwellian soldiers. Two nuns, Sister Honoria Bourke and Sister Honoria Magaen, were treated brutally. Honoria Bourke was the daughter of Richard an Iarainn (Iron Dick), second husband of Granuaile and stepsister of Tiobóid Na Long, who is buried at Ballintubber abbey. The two nuns, who were both over one hundred years old, fled to Oileán na Naoimh in Lough Furnace. They were later captured, stripped naked, had their ribs broken, and were left to die.

During the seventeenth century, several edicts were decreed, ordering the friars to quit Burrishoole. Some were driven out, while others remained, living for the most part in mud cabins in close proximity to the abbey. The friars had opened a school at Burrishoole in 1642. The college operated in times of extreme difficulty until 1697, and because of the persecution they encountered, it was sometimes necessary to conduct their schooling at hidden locations in the woods. Among the professors to teach at Burrishoole was Fr John O'Ruane and Fr Walter Jennings. The friars were expelled again in 1698 but returned in 1702. They watched the abbey fall into ruin, and in 1793 the roof eventually caved in and the friars left and were not to return. Quiet now, with its image mirrored on calm waters, its placid exterior belies its turbulent and truculent history.

The remains of Fr Manus McSweeney are buried within the walls of the abbey. He is fondly remembered in a ballad in the North Mayo Gaeltacht with the following words, 'Tá a cholainn sa talamh is a anam i bhflaitheas.' (His body is in the earth, but his soul is in paradise.)

Mulranny is an extremely pleasant place with a beautiful bay. The great hotel, built to accommodate visitors who arrived by the recently established railway, still stands above the bay, and the town has expanded a little with new houses. Like Achill, it has not yet been destroyed by over-building, with its silent villages of triangular houses that are occupied infrequently.

There is a tropical quality to the growth here, and it has the appearance of a lush Mediterranean cove when summer arrives. In winter one beds down against the storms and the heavy winds that blow in from the Atlantic. At night the lights of the southern and western coast of Clew Bay run like amber beads on the lower reaches of darkness. The traveller should rest at Mulranny. Ahead lies the Corraun Peninsula, and the dramatic island of Achill.

Once upon a time the road to Achill was almost impossible to navigate. Now one gets there with ease. The Corraun road will eventually take you to Achill Sound. The Corraun Peninsula runs at the base of Corraun Hill and is almost circular in shape. The road holds very close to the edge of the land but possesses a commanding view of Clare Island and the wide Atlantic. It is a lonely place, with the sea beetling at the base of the great cliffs. It is a place of physical tension and turmoil and suited to the solitary heart. A drive around the Corraun Peninsula brings you through the village of Corraun. The surrounding area contains many historic sites, including a shell midden site indicating that Stone Age people lived here some 5,000 years ago. The remains of a nineteenth-century copper mine can also be found here. A variety of blanket bog types are present on this peninsula.

For the walker, it is uncluttered by traffic and the views are vast and the colours subdued. The heavy waves rolling in from the heart of the Atlantic beat incessantly at the fortress cliffs of this peninsula. Irish was once spoken here, and occasionally still is. But it gradually decays and thus the remnants of a remarkable culture disappear from the landscape.

As the road swings north, the imposing profile of Achill Island points towards the west. At its southern tip lies Achill's little sister, Achillbeg.

Achill Sound runs from south to north and is a dangerous place to navigate, but for those who know the shallows and the sandbanks it shortens the trip. The whitewashed houses of Achill shine out against the backdrop of the island. High hills and mountains push directly skywards; we see Croaghaun, Slievemore, Knockmore, Deereen.

You cross into the island at Achill Sound. Much has been written concerning Achill, and writers, artists and musicians find their way there. It has been recorded in words, paintings and music. It has become a haven for creative endeavour, particularly thanks to the Heinrich Böll centre, which the man himself bequeathed to the county.

Heinrich Böll was born in Germany in 1917 and won the Nobel Prize for Literature in 1972. He carved out a career as a journalist and writer, and in the late 1950s made his first visit to Achill. Throughout the 1960s and into the 1970s, Böll lived and worked in Achill, residing in a cottage in the village of Dugort. His *Irisches Tagebuch*, or 'Irish Journal', is well known and recounts some of his experiences on Achill. The Böll Cottage in Dugort has been used as an artist's residence since 1992. His *Irisches Tagebuch* has been instrumental in bringing German people to Ireland and Achill. They still follow his dream. He came from Europe with terrible memories of the war and found tranquillity here.

As mentioned previously, throughout the 1960s and into the 1970s, Böll lived and worked in Achill, residing in a cottage in the village of Dugort. A local committee, the Heinrich Böll Foundation in Germany, the Böll family, and Mayo County Council maintain the cottage and administer the residency programme. His delightful *Irisches Tagebuch* remains a classic. It is filled with joy, as he found himself on the very edge of Europe and away from the confusion following the Second World War:

> Sitting here by the fire it is possible to play truant from Europe, while Moscow has lain in darkness for the past four hours, Berlin for two, even Dublin for half an hour: there is still a clear light over the sea, and the Atlantic persistently carries away piece by piece the Western bastion of Europe; rocks fall into the sea, soundlessly the bog streams carry the dark European soil out into the Atlantic; over the years, gently splashing, they smuggle whole fields out into the open sea, crumb by crumb.
>
> (Böll, H., *Irish Journal*. Vintage: London, 1995.)

The railway terminus ends at Achill Sound. It was only open for a short time and began and ended with tragedy. The first tragedy occurred in 1894, when thirty-two people lost their lives when the boat they were on capsized near the quays at Westport Harbour. The Achill people were on their way to Scotland to work in the potato fields. This tragedy is known as the Clew Bay Disaster. Tragedy struck again in 1937 when ten boys were burnt to death as they lay asleep in their quarters in Scotland. There were no survivors of this fire. They are buried in Kildownet cemetery with the victims of the first disaster. In 1934, the passenger service was closed, although it was reopened temporarily in 1936 while road repairs were in progress. Only freight trains continued to run until 1937. In 1937, when the Kirkintilloch Disaster claimed ten Achill victims, trains ran again to take the bodies home.

In 1886, the construction of the Achill Sound Bridge began, and one year later it was completed. The bridge was named after Michael Davitt. Prior to this people crossed the channel by ferry, which was not very safe due to the strong currents and winds. When the tide was low, people would cross the channel by foot or on horseback through shallow waters, although there were cases of people and horses being drowned due to the fast tidal surge. The bridge served the people well, but had to be rebuilt later to cope with the press of traffic. This is what Samuel Lewis had to say concerning the matter in 1837:

> This district comprehends the islands of Achill and Achillbeg, and the peninsula of Coraan [*sic*] Achill.
>
> The island of Achill, which is the largest off the Irish coast, is situated in the Atlantic Ocean, and is separated from the mainland by a narrow sound, of which the southern part, at a place called Pollranney, is fordable at low water. The western side is mostly a precipitous range of cliffs, but the eastern is in every part well sheltered. Achill Head, a bold promontory, is situated on the south-western extremity of the island and at the northern extremity is Saddle Head, at the entrance of Blacksod Bay. Between this and the smaller island of Achillbeg, which is described under its own head, is a channel called Achill Hole, where vessels drawing ten or twelve feet of water may ride in safety in all states of the weather.
>
> The peninsula of Coraan Achill, also called the Hook of Achill, lies to the east of the island, and is connected with the mainland by the narrow isthmus of Pollranney; a powerful tide runs in the sound at the narrows called the Bull's Mouth. The surface is very elevated, rising into lofty eminences, of which the highest is the hill of Coraan, 2,254 feet above the level of the sea. Keel is a coast-guard station, and is one of the six that constitute the district of Newport; and at Dugrath there is another, which is one of the six included in the district of Belmullet. The living is a rectory, in the diocese of Tuam, and in the patronage of the Archbishop: the tithes amount to £100. There is neither church, glebe-house, nor glebe: divine service is performed at the house of Achill mission, at Dugarth, twice every Sunday, in the English and Irish languages. In the R.C. divisions this forms a separate and distinct parish: there are two places of worship, one at Kildavnet and the other at Dookenella, but no regular chapel has been built.
>
> (Lewis, S., *Topographical Dictionary of Mayo*. Kennikat Press: New York, 1970.)

Robert Lloyd Praeger was born in 1869 and died in 1935. His contribution to the natural history of Ireland is of major significance. His survey of

Clare Island is regarded as a classic for its method and precision. He is best remembered for his book *The Way I Went*, which is a delightful account of his trip around Ireland. Here is what he says about Achill:

This brings us to Achill (Acaill, eagle, from *aquila*), an island only in name, for a narrow passage which cuts it off from Caurraun [*sic*] is crossed by a substantial bridge. Achill, windswept and bare, heavily peat-covered, with great gaunt brown mountains rising here and there, and a wild coast hammered by the Atlantic waves on all sides but the east, has a strange charm which everyone feels but none can fully explain. Formerly you journeyed to Achill Sound by train, when a horse-drawn vehicle ordered for the occasion jolted you nine miles through the bogs to Dugort, on the northern shore, where alone you could stay ... The ascent of Slievemore from Dugort is easy, and you obtain a bird's eye view over the whole island and a vast extent of sea and intricate coast besides. But Croaghaun in the extreme west is the finer hill. Go up by Dooagh past Lough Acorrymore lying in its great coomb, to the summit and you find yourself on the edge of a two-mile-long precipice dropping sheer into the Atlantic. Turn to the left and you descend to the far-projecting knife-edge of Achill Head – a savage place, and for the scramble to its extremities you should have nailed shoes and a good head. Or turn to the right from the summit of Croaghaun and you can visit Bunnafreeva Lough, perched on the edge of the huge cliff with another cliff overhanging it – a place so lonely and sterile and primitive that you might expect to see the piast or another water-monster rising from the inky depths of the tarn. Thence away over undulating shorn heath to Saddle Head, then eastward to two romantic lakes which lie close to the northern shore, and so back to Dooagh. This last is to my mind one of the most exhilarating walks in Ireland, with its combination of mountain and ocean and short springy turf wedged with tall cliffs or foam-fringed rocks. But what is perhaps the finest view in Achill can be obtained with the expenditure of energy required for the ascent of Croaghaun. Take the path from Dooagh along the steep hillside to the lovely little sheltered sand bay of Keem. And from there climb up the left-hand slope to the old coast-guard watchtower, and walk westward along the edge of the thousand-foot precipice; you will obtain changing and ever-wonderful views of the wild cliffs of Achill Head which will remain long in your memory.

(Praeger, R.L., *The Way That I Went*. Collins Press: Cork, 1998.)

Paul Henry, the landscape and figure painter, another fan of the island, celebrated Achill and the west of Ireland like no other artist ever did. His luminous landscapes, his great banks of white and grey clouds, his blue mountains, tawny bogs and dark pools, give his paintings a distinct quality. In 1910, he went on holidays to Achill Island and was so captivated by the people, their ways and their landscape that he decided to remain there for a period. He recorded his feelings for the island in his book, *An Irish Portrait*. Shortly after arriving in Achill he took his return rail ticket to London out of his pocket and tore it into small pieces and scattered the fragments into the sea, 'I was in the grip of something that could not be argued about, something that would not be denied, I wanted to stay in Achill, and whatever reason seemed to be against such a plan was swept aside by my overpowering desire.'

Graham Green also visited the island. He wrote parts of the novels *The Heart of the Matter* and *The Fallen Idol* in the village of Dooagh. Graham Greene retained a special affection for Achill Island, which he mentioned frequently in his letters and notes, although this was largely due to the circumstances of his visits. Graham Greene was introduced to Achill by his mistress, Catherine Walston. It was a tempestuous love affair. This story is told in the foreword to *The Third Woman* by William Cash.

One could speak endlessly of Achill and of the characters who have visited and fallen in love with it. Achill in summer, Achill in autumn, Achill in winter and Achill when the short days wheel around to spring; it has its charm at all times of the year. The island has a long history which begins when the first Stone Age travellers beached their leather boats on the white strand at Keem Bay. They say that the Phoenicians anchored their ships here as they sought the purple dye from the whelks that abounded here. They came when the Mediterranean had been emptied of these whelks.

Grace O'Malley owned a castle at Kildavnet. It was more a tower house than a castle and could have been built by one of her ancestors. It is strategically placed at the entrance to Achill Sound. Tower houses are fortified residences of stone (usually four or more stories high), which were erected by both Anglo-Normans and Gaelic families in Ireland, between 1400 and 1650.

The front cover of Theresa McDonald's impressive book on Achill features a coloured print of the famous mission on Achill. In the nineteenth century a Church of Ireland minister, the Reverend Edward Nangle, set up a mission in Dugort with the purpose of converting the people of Achill to the Protestant faith. He was an intense man, a man of deep personal piety, self-denial and sacrifice, but also impulsive and obstinate. The project ran for almost fifty years, and Nangle built schools, cottages, an orphanage, a small hospital and the island's first hotel (now the Slievemore). During the famine years, the Colony, as it was known, offered soup to the starving islanders in return for converting to the Protestant faith. The Colony was very successful for a time and regularly produced a newspaper called *The Achill Missionary Herald*. The Reverend Nangle expanded his mission into Mweelin, where a 'school' was built. The Achill Mission began to decline slowly after Nangle was moved from Achill and was finally closed in the 1880s. Edward Nangle died in 1883. His achievements were quite incredible and never properly praised. He took the side of a barren hillside, made it fertile, built proper houses, produced a newspaper, educated children and gave people a good life. In the following pastoral description of the area we get some idea of the changes he wrought on the landscape:

> A small field of oats was reaped on our mission far, the grain of the finest quality. The ground where it grew was a useless bog three years ago. A limestone quarry which a friend lately discovered in the immediate neighbourhood of our Settlement, will greatly forward our agricultural work, as we find by experience that lime is the best manure for the bog-land, indeed it cannot be effective reclaimed without it. Our potato crop is remarkably productive, and we are happy to say that it is generally so throughout the island.
> (Quoted by Theresa McDonald. *The Achill Missionary Herald 1837*. I.A.S. Publications, 1997.)

There was much tension lying beneath it all. The Reverend Edward Nangle is reported to have said upon his death bed, 'Achill may well be called the Happy Valley. In spite of all our trials, I know no place like it.'

The Road to Belmullet

We return to Mulranny and set off towards Belmullet. As you drive around the bend, the muted green, brown and purple landscape opens before you into boggy terrain with solitary lakes. The landscape possesses the muted colours of bogland. It seems to stretch for ever.

The bogs were once a source of fuel. During the most difficult of centuries, people cut this turf, which took 10,000 years to form, and within which is preserved the natural history of Ireland. You will still see people cutting turf in the Mayo countryside. The deeper you cut down in a bank of turf the darker the fuel becomes because of the pressure. Turf is usually cut with a slane. The sods are placed on the bank to dry. They lie in the sun, which hardens the skin. They are turned until the skin is formed and the sod has grown smaller but more solid. Then it is placed in 'Groogeens' and is later stacked neatly by the side of the road in well-formed piles, with the sods set at a slight angle so that the rain runs down to the ground and never enters the heart of the pile. It is then carried home.

That is the classical way to do things but you will rarely see this stack of turf anymore, so familiar from Paul Henry drawings. White and yellow plastic bags are now used. In the Midlands, they have great machines for processing the turf and even in Mayo they have sausage machines that delve lightly into the earth and produce tubes of turf. This savaging of bogs means that the fauna and the flora of the countryside are being quietly destroyed. But at this late hour, efforts are being made to preserve some of these natural resources. Sphagnum moss is one of the few plants that like the wet acid bogs. It can grow in the bog, trapping water in its spongy body. Each Sphagnum plant can hold up to twenty times its own weight in water. Different species of Sphagnum moss cover the surface of the bogs. Some live in bog pools, while others prefer to be drier, on the tops of small hummocks.

New development.

The carpet of moss covering the bog is full of subtle colours: greens, reds, yellows, oranges and ginger browns. This soft squidgy carpet is where other bog plants are found. These bogs are a living carpet of colour and the road to Belmullet is a natural tapestry of these subdued tones. You will find dark bog pools everywhere. Bogs are natural reservations and are ideal for birds. Wading birds like snipe, golden plover, and curlew, nest and feed in the bogland. In summer they probe into the soft peat looking for food. All day long the skylark sings over the bog. In the winter, bogs are feeding and roosting sites for Arctic geese (known as Greenland white-fronted geese), and for birds of prey such as the kestrel and merlin. The red grouse spends its entire year on the open bogs, raising chicks in the summer months. They gather in family flocks in the autumn and over winter on the bogs.

Here and there a green, well-cultivated drumlin rises from the bog. There is firm habitation, here with houses which show brightly above the brown plain of turf. There are a number of remains of fishing or hunting lodges hidden within protective and sometimes exotic trees. Once, these were rich with wildfowl and the rivers carried a plentiful supply of fish. The eastern rim of this wide bogscape is bordered by the Nephin Beg range. Even on the lower slopes of these weathered mountains the eye discovers cottages and farms. The most striking feature of the landscape are the lakes, carrying the reflection of the clouds on a clear day, or stretches of heather and delicate bog cotton. Sometimes the rains sweep across these wide spaces, blocking vision, sometimes a rich rainbow arches across the bogs, lodging its base in the mountains. Sometimes on a summer's day, lazy and cotton-light clouds move slowly across the sky. This is Ireland's largest bog.

This is how Praeger saw this landscape in 1937:

> Indeed the Nephin Beg range of mountains is I think the very loneliest place in the country, for the hills themselves are encircled by this vast area of trackless bog. Where else even in Ireland will you find 200 square miles which is houseless and roadless – nothing but brown heather spreading as far as you can see, and rising along a kind of central backbone into high bare hills breaking down here and there in rocky scarps, with the Atlantic winds singing along their slopes? I confess I find such a place not lonely or depressing but inspiring. You are thrown at the same time back upon yourself and forward against the mystery and majesty of nature, and you may feel dimly something of your own littleness and your own greatness; for sure man is as great as he is little; but the littleness is actual, and the greatness largely potential.
>
> (Praeger, R.L., *The Way That I Went*. The Collins Press: Cork, 1947.)

The first town one encounters is at Ballycroy. Firm trees define the place, together with honeysuckle. Bogland landscape runs towards the distant mountains. People have lived in this landscape for a very long time. If we are to judge by the evidence of the Céide fields, it is possible they were here during the early Stone Age.

One takes the white road defined by telegraph poles to Bangor. For the old storytellers of the area this spare and empty landscape is invested with magic, mayhem, murder, lust, love, a great march, and a great battle for this vast area is the location of the forgotten saga called *Táin Bó Flidhais*.

The coast road to Belmullet.

Táin Bó Flidhais

For many a storyteller or 'seanchaí' of North Mayo, the great saga *Táin Bó Flidhais* ends close to Carrowmore Lake. It was here that Fergus MacRóigh killed his wife Flidhais in a river flowing out of the lake. It is a curtain-raiser to the Táin saga and some of the monumental characters from that epic appear in this story, including the great Maedbh herself.

The story concerns heroine Flidhais Fholtchain, or 'Flidhais of the lovely soft hair', her luckless husband Oilill Fionn, a king of the Gamhanraidh, her legendary maol (hornless cow), which could satisfy three hundred men in one milking, together with women and children. The story tells of Flidhais's lust for the handsome, deceitful and belligerent former king of Ulster Fergus Mac Róigh and the terrible consequences of this illicit and earthy union. The intrigue was brought about by the great manipulator and moral delinquent Bricne.

Flidhais was a ravishingly beautiful woodland goddess, who drove a chariot driven by deer. She was known for having an affair with Fergus MacRóich, whose sexual appetite only she could satisfy. She has often been compared to the Roman Diana and the Greek Artemis. *Táin Bó Fladhais* is a tale of intrigue, feasting, revenge, fearful battles, mindless slaughter, burnings and great marches. It possesses a raw pagan quality and is indeed very ancient. It is quite racy and gives a mythological cloak to this bleak landscape of North Mayo. It is one of these great Mayo stories that has fallen out of general memory except with storytellers in North Mayo. To the informed storyteller, every townland, hill and fort in this area has mythological associations.

We now pass through Bangor. The name Bangor comes from the Irish Beann Chor which means 'Ridge of Mountain Peaks'. Major Bingham, having inherited almost half of Erris from his mother, formerly Frances Shaen, came to live here in around 1796. After he married Elizabeth Nash of Cloonatilla he settled at Bangor and built a dwelling house on a hillside overlooking the road. It was at the crossroads of two old roads that had been in use since the mid-eighteenth century. Bingham transformed the town. In around 1798 he introduced the Revenue Police in an effort to stamp out the distillation of poitín. The barracks was built from local stone and was roofed with thick stone slabs from Glenturk. Bingham, having founded the town, was determined not to allow the construction of a Catholic church here, but this prohibition on Catholic churches ended when Robert Savage, who had married one of the Bingham ladies, gave permission for the erection of a church in Ballybeg, the neighbouring townland. A thatched building was built as a chapel as close to the town as possible, on the site where the present Catholic church is built.

One has a choice at Bangor Cross. To the west lies Gweesalia where John Millington Synge is said to have based his play *The Playboy of the Western World*.

Doohooma is a village situated approximately fifteen miles south-west of Bangor Erris, overlooking Achill Island to the south. The Doohooma Peninsula is almost an island. It is connected to the mainland of Erris only by a narrow spit at Gweesalia. It was originally known in old Irish as *Dumhaigh Thuama*, meaning the 'sounding sandy banks'. In an area noted for its outstanding natural beauty, Doohooma is particularly impressive, with an extensive panorama of sea, sky and mountain surrounding it on every side. To the south, Achill Island lies a few miles across, with Sliabh Mór and the towering cliffs of Achill Head dominating the southern horizon. To the west of Doohooma Head lie the islands of the Iniskeas and Duvillan.

Each year workers used to leave this area and go in search of work in Scotland and northern England. They took the ship at Doohooma Head and sailed away to hard work, rough conditions and low pay. They saved their money and sent it home.

Doohooma is situated fifteen miles southwest of Bangor Erris, overlooking Achill Island to the south. There was a ferry service from the neighbouring village, Tallaghan Bawn, to Ballycroy, throughout the nineteenth and early part of the twentieth century. Regular visits were made across the bay for social functions as well as trade purposes. General goods were traded between this port and the towns of Westport and Newtown. The channel can be dangerous and the *Harlequin* was wrecked in December 1823 while making this crossing.

Bellacorrick is marked by the peat-generating station. It looks visionary and misplaced, but for over forty years it has generated electricity. It is now silent, and the bog has returned to its natural form. It no longer feeds the great furnaces to generate electricity. It was a brave effort and did well in its time, bringing hope to the region before the 'Celtic Tiger' began to roar. The first windmills in Ireland were built there in 1992. The wind is steady and the ground is flat, with an open aspect to the prevailing winds. The turf cutter will continue to cut the turf in the old-fashioned way, with his slane, setting it to dry in the sun.

Bellacorrick is famous for its stone bridge. It is built across the Abhann Mhór and separates Erris from the rest of the world, or so they say. When an emigrant passed over the bridge he knew he was home, and the wonder of his world stretched before him. Everyone rubs a stone on the surface of the bridge, for it rings with music; why it should do this no one knows. There is a block missing on the bridge and they say that one of the men who built on the bridge died after working on it, and they also say that whoever replaces the stone block will die.

The prophet Brian Rua is associated with this area. One of his prophesies is very familiar all over Mayo. They say that he predicted that one day news would travel faster on poles from Dublin to Blacksod Bày than a hawk could fly. He wrote a book of prophesies but he threw it into a lake in the area and there it lies, with all its hidden secrets. He was called Brian Rua because of his red hair and he lived and died in the seventeenth century.

The islands off the coast are sacred, and the monks in their canvas currachs sailed past Annagh Head, Eagle Island, Erris Head, the Stags of Broad Haven, and across Donegal Bay to the island of Iona and Lindisfarne. St Brendan was not the only navigator who passed up this coast. After the debacle for the Irish at the Synod of Whitby, the monks led by St Colmán left Lindisfarne and travelled down the western sea lanes on their way to Inishbofin. St Brendan will turn up again later and I will expand upon his importance then.

There is local evidence that Synge stayed in Gweesalia and in Belmullet, where Jack B. Yeats was a guest of his at the Erris Hotel in Belmullet. It is widely acknowledged that part of the plot of *The Playboy of the Western World* came from an anecdote that Synge heard from an old man in the Aran Islands. Synge records the source of the story in his book, *The Aran Islands.*

The story is that of James Lynchehaun, who assaulted his employer, an English lady, on Achill Island, and was sheltered from the police by the people. He then escaped to America and became a folk hero. His fascinating life is recorded in James Carney's *The Playboy and The Yellow Lady.*

In 1715, Sir Arthur Shaen began building a small town on a wet and marshy area near the 'Mullet' peninsula in the extreme north-west of the barony of Erris. Early in the nineteenth century, Belmullet consisted of just a few thatched buildings, and it was not until 1820 that the first post office in the Erris region was opened, while in 1822 the coastguard was established in the town. The new road between Belmullet and Castlebar was completed in 1824. The famous and impressive Erris Hotel was built from granite and sandstone carried from Blacksod. In 1826, a quay large enough to accommodate vessels of one hundred tons was built. This helped to accelerate the importation of goods, especially from Britain, which now included tea, sugar, beer, wine, coal and grain. During the 1820s it was a lively place. Roads were opening up and making communication easier, and agriculture in the area was developing at a fast pace. In the outlying districts land was being reclaimed, and there was a general feeling of optimism about these years.

We read the following in Kathleen Villiers-Tuthill's biography of Alexander Nimmo:

> Cartherr instructed Knight to build a pier at Belmullet. Nimmo, on viewing the pier while under construction, declared it inadequate for the needs of the town and he convinced The Fishery Board to issue funds, in addition to a similar contribution from Carter, to complete the works to a more satisfactory state. Knight decided to take the task even further and to contribute funds of his own to ensure that the pier at Belmullet would have been of similar standard, if not superior to any other on the peninsula. The town developed rapidly and by 1824 boasted a store, several small shops, and almost all of the building lots had been taken. The store was full with oats and barley and two cargoes had already been shipped that season.
> (Villiers-Tuthill, K., *Alexander Nimmo and the Western District*. Connemara Girl Publications: Connemara, 2006.)

Alexander Nimmo, was a pioneering Scottish engineer who came to Ireland in 1811. His many reports to the Bog Commission and the Fishery Board give us a invaluable picture of conditions on the west coast during the early years of the nineteenth century.

You next cross the Belmullet Swing Bridge. The road north leads to Broad Haven Bay, Erris Head, and Eagle Island with its lighthouse. This is rugged terrain, sometimes shrouded in mist, sometimes troubled by howling storms, sometimes quiet and gentle with a blue sky above. This part of the island is broad and protected by cliffs. As you go south, the land grows flatter, with small hills and sand dunes tightened by marram grass.

At Cross cemetery, Ríocarde Bairéid is buried. He was born in Barrack in 1740 and lived in the area all of his life, working as a small farmer and as a teacher. He was a renowned storyteller and raconteur who was very popular with the local gentry. He is famous for having written *Preab san Ól* and a savage mock lament for a bailiff in his poem 'Eoin Cóir' or 'Righteous John'.

Off the coast of Belmullet lie the Iniskea Islands. These islands have been settled for 4,000 years and there have been several different settlements on the islands during this time. The Bronze Age people made their mark here, as did the ancient monks. Evidence found here suggests the monks manufactured ink to produce the Irish manuscripts of that era and that they lived in beehive huts. They abandoned the islands in the twelfth century.

In the eighteenth century it was re-inhabited because of pressure on the land. The people who now settled here were hard-working and prosperous. They planted potatoes, wheat and barley and were engaged in fishing. They sold salted mackerel and herring to the townspeople of Belmullet and Westport. Owing to their relative isolation, they had little interference from landlords. They didn't have their own supply of turf but traded their goods with Achill for it.

At this time Iniskea was renowned for the quality of its poitín. Captain Boycott's wife refused to drink any other kind, and Maxwell, writing in the 1820s, said that the islanders should be canonised, such was the calibre of their brew. One barrel of the famous poitín was worth a year's rent.

Though all the islanders were Catholic, they were extremely superstitious. They had a large stone called the Naomh Óg, which they wrapped in clothing and venerated. They would bring it out during storms and dip it into the sea during prayer meetings. A priest who came from the mainland to try to stop this practice was so annoyed at his failure to do so that he broke the stone. It is said that he suffered bad luck for the rest of his life.

In the 1920s a Norwegian whaling station was established on the south island. The whales were used to make oils and other by-products. In October 1927, tragedy struck Iniskea, when a severe storm hit the islands and twelve young men were entangled in their fishing nets and drowned. It was the beginning of the end for the island and the last inhabitant left in 1934.

The island of Inishglora is steeped in legends and traditions. The most widely known is that of the Children of Lir, who were changed into swans by their evil stepmother and condemned to spend 300 years on Lough Derravarragh, 300 years on the Sea of Moyle and finally 300 years on the Atlantic, off the Erris coast. There are various versions of this story. The end of their sentence coincided with Brendan's arrival on Inishglora. Every Sabbath they attended Mass there, sitting on the roof of Teampall na bhFear, and each time the host was raised, they drooped their wings and bent their necks. Such devotion did not go unrewarded. They were baptised by Brendan and regained their human shape, but only briefly, before they crumbled to dust.

Belmullet to Ballina

You leave Belmullet and travel towards Barr na Trá. Shore fishing is particularly good all around this area. The miles of accessible coastline and almost deserted beaches guarantee perfect peace. Naturalists are attracted to this remote place. There are over thirty-nine varieties of fish known to inhabit the waters off the shores of Belmullet. Early March brings Glaucous and Iceland Gulls, and sometimes Thayer's Gull. This gull, which breeds in Arctic Canada but normally winters on the Pacific coast of America, has become an almost annual visitor to Ireland. Less rare, but still interesting, gull records include two Kumlien's Gulls as well as thirteen Iceland Gulls at Barr na Trá.

This area was never disconnected from the world. It was an important and active sea lane. The coastline has served as a graveyard for many fine vessels. In his book, Fr Seán Noone's writes of the area:

Inver was well known to the Spaniards. For many years before and after the Armada, Spanish vessels used Broadhaven Bay. Captain Charles Plessington, an English coastguard reported to Sir Robert Cecil, Queen Elizabeth's private secretary on July 1601, 'I found out the place where the Spaniards, at their first arrival, do harbour themselves to learn news and take in pilots. This river is upon the westernmost part of Connaught, between Cape Achill and Cape Killala, whereof lie certain rocks called the Stages, from which the river runs into the country of the O'Bourkes, due South and North. I know no name for it yet. But hither came two ships from Spain with treasure and munitions at Christmas last. Here they stayed a fortnight and from whence they went to Teelin and Killybegs and there remained one month in discharging of their loading.
(Noone, Fr S., *Where The Sun Sets, a History of North Mayo*. Erris Publications: Mayo.)

The Irish names of the headlands and villages run mellifluously off the tongue. Kid Island, Benwee Head, Doonvinalla, Portacloy, Illanmaster, Ceathrú Taidhg and many others, all hark back to an earlier tongue and earlier names for landmarks.

One passes on to Glenamoy. The Glenamoy River, which rises east of Glencalry and close to Benmore Mountain, is a salmon and sea trout river. Spread across this area are hunting lodges which one comes upon unexpectedly. In the nineteenth and early twentieth centuries they were strange, cultivated islands on wide stretches of bog.

We leave this peaceful area and travel towards Belderg. It stands grandly above the sea. From this vantage point one can look across Donegal Bay to the Donegal mountains. Beneath, the eternal waves eat away at the tall, layered headlands and cliffs. The sound of the beating waves is carried up the cliffs to the viewing platform, and below the seagulls turn or glide on quiet wings.

What brought this area to prominence was the archaeological work done by Patrick Caulfield and his son Michael. Patrick had noted that beneath the bog cover and down some ten feet lay well-formed wall patterns, which had collapsed. His son Michael, who was an archaeologist, began a dig in the area. What he discovered beneath the bog was a well-ordered walled field system that is over 5,000 years old. The archaeological world took notice of this and it changed their whole perception of early European farming.

The farming revolution started in the Fertile Crescent 10,000 years ago, and here was evidence that it flourished in Ireland 500 or 600 years later. The Céide Fields demonstrated a well-established society. This society consisted of

The Céide Fields.

Cliffscapes of Céide Fields.

a community of farmers working peacefully together, clearing the forest for land, raising their cattle and setting their seed crops on lazy beds. Lazy beds, as they are called, are used to this day in Ireland and are a most efficient way of setting potatoes. The discovery has changed our whole way of looking at the lives of Stone Age man.

Set about the area are megalithic tombs, which suggest that a coherent and sophisticated religious and social structure was in place. It also asks the more interesting question as to how they got here. Did they travel up from Spain in great leather boats? If they did, they must have moved slowly, first settling in Kerry, Clare, Galway, and Mayo. Or did they pass over from Scotland and move across the country? The alignment of the megalithic tombs seems to suggest that they landed on the western coast. It is speculation at the moment, but genetic fingerprinting may reveal something more definite.

The question of who the original inhabitants of the Céide Fields were still remains open. Having studied part of the walled system and puzzled about figures emerging from the mists of time, one travels on to Belderg proper. Across this whole area one can find reminders of the megalithic past, such as court tombs, portal tombs, wedge-shaped tombs, standing stones bearing Ogham inscriptions, ancient churches and ring forts.

Peter and Margo Maxwell had an artistic dream in 1992. They decided to build an artistic centre close to the sea and to invite artists to work at the Ballinglen Centre on Main Street. Artists from all over the world come to this area to study the landscape and reinterpret it. Art shaped and inspired here has been curated all over the world.

This foundation is of international importance and is based in the town of Ballycastle. The next stop on the way should be Kilcummin. There was great excitement on 22 August 1798, when 1,000 French soldiers under General Jean Joseph Amable Humbert landed in the north-west of the country, at Kilcummin in Co. Mayo. The story of what happened next is set out in a recent book by Stephen Dunford and Guy Beiner, entitled *In Humbert's Footsteps*. The whole event did not last very long. It started at Kilcummen and ended on the bloody battlefield at Ballinamuck. This is how an eyewitness described the scene:

> A serene and cloudless sky, and brilliant sun, rendered 22 of August one of the finest days of that remarkable season. It was on the morning of that day, whilst proceeding from Palmerstown to Killala, I first beheld a ship of war; three vessels of unusual size, magnified by the still calm of the ocean, stretched slowly across the bay at Rathfran (on the larboard tack) weathering the reef which divides it from the bay at Killala.
> (Dunford, S., *In Humbert's Footsteps. Mayo 1798*. Fadó Books: Dublin, 2006.)

Napoleon then intervened and dispatched an army to Ireland, and after fifteen days at sea they arrived at Kilcummin, having moved rapidly. As Humbert moved towards Killala, news quickly passed through the countryside and his small force was joined by Irish rebels. Humbert was thirty-two when he undertook the expedition, and a veteran of many campaigns.

The next town taken was Killala, and the town remained under Franco-Irish rule for thirty-two days, until the British army defeated the French army in battle and executed the local Irish rebels. The expedition was short, forceful, and, in the end, a disaster.

Ballina was later captured, and the army moved towards Castlebar by taking a tortuous route through the mountains. On 27 August Castlebar was taken. Here, Humbert proclaimed the Republic of Connaught and set up John Moore as its first president. In the meantime the English army were given time to regroup and at the final Battle of Ballinamuck the whole endeavour faltered and failed. The French were treated decently and as prisoners of war; the Irish rebels, however, were pursued and butchered.

The foundation of the diocese of Killala dates from the time of St Patrick, who placed his disciple St Muredach here. Muredach is described as an old

The Ballinglen Arts Foundation, brainchild of Peter and Margo Maxwell.

The view from the Arts Centre in Ballycastle.

Fishing boats at anchor in Killala.

Killala Harbour.

Protestant church in Killala.

Round Tower in Killala.

man of Patrick's family, and he was appointed to the church of Killala as early as 442 or 443. It is probable that he gave up his seat after a few years, and retired to end his life on the lonely island in Donegal Bay that has since borne his name: Innismurray.

It was at Killala that Patrick baptised the two maidens whom he had met during his childhood at Focluth Wood by the western sea, whose voices at night had often sadly called for him to come and dwell amongst them once more. He did come, baptised them, and built them a church, where they spent the rest of their days.

Along the left bank of the gentle River Moy lie the ruins of several monasteries. They are all close to the sea, with good land to sustain them, and they possess an air of calm and tranquillity. This present tranquillity can give us a false impression of their history. Rosserk, a Franciscan house, was founded in 1460. The beautiful Abbey of Moyne still stands, in almost perfect condition, on a scenic site just over the river, and further on, north of Killala, stands the Dominican Abbey of Rathfran. Until quite recently, another monastery, on the promontory of Errew, running into Lough Conn, was

Ballylahan Castle; the Norman presence.

occupied. An impressive round tower in Killala itself, still perfectly preserved, is evidence of the ancient importance of the place as an ecclesiastical centre.

This part of the journey ends at Killala. Killala is neatly arranged with some fine buildings. The gaunt castles of Grace O'Malley are left behind in another century, and fine eighteenth-century houses are evident in this town. The French officers occupied the palace of the Protestant bishop, where they lived for a short time with his lordship and family.

Ballina to Castlebar

The land on the way to Ballina is fertile. The landscape changes as one travels this way. It is gentle and easy, and a far cry from the harsh hills and empty spaces of the Erris peninsula. One appreciates wide Killala Bay with its lazy sea shallows, its tranquil tides, and its sense of indolence even more after passing through harder country.

There had been early Patrician foundations here, but it was with the coming of the Normans that the great abbeys and churches were built. The new foundations were founded by the new Continental orders. They were built as the Dark Ages were coming to an end. Rosserk Abbey, the Abbey of Moyne and Rathfran are testament to the vigour of the new religious orders established in Europe.

Rathfran

The history of Rathfran belongs to the Dominican order. This friary was founded in 1274 and may have been founded by the De Exeters, who were a Norman family who later changed their names to Jordan. The fact that St Dominic died in 1221 means that the monastery was built shortly after the saint passed away. It would have been built in a Dominican style and would have followed the Dominican rules and regulations. The first Dominican to come to Rathfran was probably Stephen De Exeter. The ruins are well-preserved and built strongly and firmly, in sight of the tranquil sea. Its very size indicates that it would have housed many friars and guests.

Life in this monastery – the excitements, the silence, the prayers and the theological disputes – are closed to us, as very little documentary evidence remains. In the fifteenth century, indulgences were granted to the faithful who visited the church. We read in a petition from 1456 that this part of Ireland had been reduced to such misery by war and other disasters that the alms of the faithful were lacking and that the friars had neglected divine worship and were obliged to follow rural occupations. The sixteenth century brought little relief. Edmund Bourke of Castlebar was murdered here by the sons of his brother Walter.

Religious troubles in Europe, which would tear it asunder for 400 years, had a colossal effect on this quiet estuary. The monastery was suppressed. The friars at Rathfran could not withhold the powers marshalled against them. The old order was changing. In 1577, the lands and the fishing rights were leased to Thomas De Exeter and later to various others.

Moyne Abbey

This beautiful abbey is set on the shores of Killala Bay. It is a spectacular building and has stood the test of time well, for it remains in good condition today. Architecture had advanced greatly in Europe, and the great Gothic cathedrals dominated the cities and towns. So the techniques of the Gothic arch and the high arched window was well understood.

The church was consecrated in 1462. It was founded in the 1450s by the MacWilliam Burke family, or possibly by a member of the Barrett family. The windows of the church demonstrate the fine and delicate stonework of the time.

By 1500 the abbey had become a student house and there were fifty in the community. As time passed, the abbey was extended and improved. From a distance the abbey is dominated by a high tower. This was built later and the stairs leading to the top are still serviceable. The cloisters, where the friars walked, are at the very heart of the complex plan and were built in about 1500. Between 1578 and 1579 the friary was raided. Moyne Abbey was raided again by the ferocious Sir Richard Bingham in 1590. The friary was destroyed and the monks dispersed.

It is said that the soldiers tried to force the abbot to confess that he had been engaged in a plot against Queen Elizabeth. The abbot firmly denied having any knowledge of the plot. He was, however, sentenced to hanging. To this day the beautiful abbey stands firm and impressive, close to Killala Bay.

Another friary burned by Bingham is that at Rosserk, some five miles north of Ballina, which was built by the Joyce family in 1441 for the Observatine

Franciscans. It is generally considered to be the finest Franciscan construction in the country and is certainly the best preserved. It stands by the sea and has a gem-like quality. There is an impressive arched doorway and an east-facing window. The stairs from the cloisters lead up to the sleeping quarters and refectory above the vaulted rooms on the ground floor.

The following letter, sourced for the author of this book by Noel O'Neill, gives us some idea of the ecclesiastical turmoil that visited abbeys so far from Rome. The letter is dated 30 April 1460:

Mandate to the Archdeacon of Killala and William Bared and William O'Cearind, Canons of the same.

The Pope having been informed by Niallanus O'Dubda, a Canon of Killala, that Cornelius O'Buabhilid, perpetual vicar of the parish of Castleconnor, in the Diocese of Killala, an open and notorious fornicator, has committed simony and has violated an interdict lately laid by authority of the Delegate of the Apostolic See in certain places of those parts to the shame of the clerical order.

If and after Niallanus, who says he is of noble birth by both parents, accuses Cornelius before the above three, to summon Cornelius and others concerned, and if they find the charges true, or one of them enough for the purpose, to remove Cornelius and collate the vicarage, value eight marks, to Niallanus, notwithstanding that he has already been received as a Canon of Killala by authority of the Ordinary.

The Pope hereby dispenses Niallanus, who is only a clerk, not to be obliged, while studying Canon or civil law in a University or in a non-university Studium, to have himself promoted to deacon's or priest's orders for seven years, provided that, within a year of obtaining the vicarage, he is ordained sub-deacon.

(Noel O'Neill, Private Papers, Castlebar.)

Ballina stands by the majestic Moy. Here the river meets the sea. Its journey has been slow and untroubled. It drains Co. Mayo. The system includes great lakes such as the Conn and Cullin, but also many small lakes and streams. For much of its course, the Moy flows through pastureland. The Nephin Beg range stands on the western horizon and the Ox mountains mark the eastern watershed. The channel, or gut, runs for several miles before it runs into the sea beyond the slender and low-lying island of Bartragh.

Left: The stately Moy, Ballina.

Below: The River Moy in spate.

Ballina is set on old foundations, and the Dolmen at Primrose Hill, near the railway station, is evidence of this. It is known as 'the Dolmen of the Four Maols'. The Dolmen dates from about 2000 BC and is sometimes locally called 'the Table of the Giants'. It is said that the four Maols are buried underneath the Dolmen. The four Maols murdered Ceallach, a seventh-century Bishop of Connaught, and they were hanged at Ardnaree, the Hill of Executions.

For hundreds of years the annals only spoke of bloody deeds, murder, the ownership of land and the transfer of properties In 1371 Donncha Ó Dubhda single-handedly attacked the English of Tireragh and took Castleconnor and Ardnaree castles. He drove out the English living within them.

All the notes from the annals are of such a nature. In 1586 Sir Richard Bingham fought the Scots at Ardnaree, where he routed them. They had captured the

The Dolmen of the Four Maols.

castle and held it for three days. Ardnaree is on the east side of the town, and an Augustinian friary was built there in the early fifteenth century. The stylised doorway still remains, with its two finials, and a double window above.

The Belleek estate once occupied lands from the Moy River to the modern-day Killala Road. The 1798 centenary memorial, the Humbert Monument, was dedicated on 11 May 1898; it was late because the money was also being used to fund revolutionary organisations. The monument is not Humbert at all but Mother Ireland. Maud Gonne, a famous Irishwoman, unveiled the monument. At the event Maud Gonne famously poured water over another speaker's head. In 1798 the town was taken over by the French.

In this extract taken from Lewis's *Topographical Dictionary of Mayo*, he describes the commercial activity of the Ballina:

A very extensive tobacco and snuff manufactory was established in 1801, by Mr Malley, who first persevered in opening the navigation of the River Moy, and thus gave a powerful impulse to the commercial prosperity of the town: the manufacture continued to flourish, and in 1809 the duties paid to Government amounted to £8,000. In 1834, Mr J. Brennan, a merchant from Belfast, introduced the provision trade, which was previously unknown in this neighbourhood, and erected spacious premises adjoining the river, and commodious stores 350 feet long and140 feet wide, with complete apparatus adapted to a peculiar method of curing: in this concern 10,000 pigs are killed annually and after being cured are sent to London; and there are also others: which carry on an extensive provision trade. There are two large ale and porter breweries, and two large oatmeal and flour-mills. The weaving of linen is carried on to a small extent by weavers who work in their own houses. This is the principal port in the county: in 1829 there were 119 vessels, of the aggregate burden of 11,097 tons, employed in the exportation of grain to the extent, in the course of that year, of 10,831 tons of oats, 130 tons of wheat, 106 tons of barley, and 30 tons of meal; and during the same period, 66 vessels, of the aggregate burden of 5479 tons, were employed in the importation of British and foreign goods. The fishery is carried on with great success; at the falls of the river are salmon weirs, which have been rebuilt by Messrs Little, at an expense of £1,500, and in which great quantities of fish are taken and shipped for Dublin and Liverpool.

(Lewis, S., *Topographical Dictionary of Mayo*. Kennikat Press: New York, 1970.)

During the early nineteenth century the town was a hive of activity. Belleek Castle was built from cut stone during these exciting days of expansion. The manor was erected by the eldest son of James Knox, the proprietor of Mount Falcon. After the death of James Knox on 21 October 1818, his eldest son Francis Arthur Knox-Gore of Belleek Manor succeeded him and was made Baronet on 5 December 1868. The cost of erecting this magnificent castle amounted to £10,000.

He died on 21 May 1873, in the grounds of the castle. Over his resting place stands an imposing monument of cut stone, which was erected by his son Charles James. The monument is surrounded by a deep moat. Sir Charles Knox-Gore was also buried at Belleek, overlooking the river Moy. When Sir Charles died, the property was passed on to his daughter Matilda.

Belleek Castle remained the property of the Knox-Gore family for over one hundred years. However, the estate was sold to the Beckett family of Ballina in 1940. Jacob Francis Beckett had planned to turn the estate into a racecourse and stud farm but died before he could realise his dream. The Beckett family invested time and money in restoring the castle to its former glory and later sold the property to Mayo County Council. It became a sanatorium in the 1950s and it was subsequently turned into a hotel. It is an interesting hotel with a unique maritime ambience. The Captain Ward Room is constructed from oak balks salvaged from the galleons from the

Castile Squadron, a ship which was wrecked off the Atlantic Mayo coast in the seventeenth century. A magnificent collection of artefacts is exhibited, including a classic figurehead of Spanish conquistador Hernán Cortés.

The Spanish Armada was visited by all sorts of bad luck from the outset. As the remnants of the fleet made its way along the western coast of Ireland tragedy befell it. Where the soldiers and sailors of that fleet made it ashore, they were treated savagely by the Irish and the English.

It is almost time to leave Ballina, situated beside the lordly Moy, but before we leave we must mention the fact that the first woman president of Ireland, Mary Robinson, was born here on 21 May 1944. She famously put a special symbolic light in her kitchen window in Áras an Uachtaráin, which was visible to the public and was a sign of remembering Irish emigrants around the world.

The road divides outside Ballina, and heading south we take the road to Knockmore. As the name suggests, it lies beneath a great hill which is brown and purple with heather and rough commonage. You cross a railway bridge and move evenly along the road, with good land on softer hills to the right, and hard bogland to the left. At the turn of the road there was once an alcohol factory; its purpose was to turn potatoes into commercial alcohol. Beside the factory stands a house that seems more suitable to the continent of Europe of sixty years ago. It has the quality of an abstract painting. It was constructed in slabs in Holland, carried to Corroy and erected here.

Knockmore is on the shores of Lough Conn. The lake is an angler's paradise and during the fishing season there is always a boat on the lake. On dark days it lies in silhouette, with some patient fisherman and gillie waiting for a fish. It attracts anglers from all over the continent. Majestic Nephin Mountain rises firmly in the background. Nephin, observed from here, rises evenly and symmetrically out of the earth. It is a cone-shaped quartzite mountain, standing alone overlooking Lough Conn. Its contour is soft and gentle and rises to over 800 metres. It is the second highest mountain in Connaught and gently shaped. White markings run down its slopes like the beds of dried streams, and the first snow in Ireland always falls here. There is an Irish proverb that says, 'Snow on Nephin, cold in Ireland.' It is almost at the very centre of things and must have been sacred to ancient man, as was the matching mountain of Croagh Patrick.

When you cross Pontoon Bridge it is time to pause, for here the small woods cling to tough hills. Pontoon Bridge spans the cut that joins the River

Above: Lough Conn.

Left: Nephin, cloud-capped.

Below: Pontoon, in a winter mode.

Conn to the River Cullen. Sometimes the water moves one way and then it reverses and runs the other way. Artists, writers and intellectuals have been drawn by its tranquillity, and it was on the borders of this lake that Emily McManus retired from Guy's hospital. She retired to read and fish and write in her small house by the lake. She loved her county dearly. She came from a distinguished family in Mayo and led an active life. She travelled widely and became matron of Guy's hospital in London during the war. Finally, she settled into life in her little cottage beside Lough Conn:

> In this year I had begun to build a little fishing lodge for myself near Pontoon, Foxford, and only seventeen miles from Killeaden. The Land Commission were selling plots in a lovely spot where Carrickbarret Wood, one of the few remaining indigenous oak woods in Ireland, came down to the shores of Lough Conn. The son of a neighbour undertook to act as Clerk of the Works and manager to a batch of local labourers, here mother and I were the joint architects, and in autumn the work began on my site, a small rocky hill

Lough Conn, with Nephin in the background.

overlooking the little road, the bog and Lough Conn just beyond it. In lovely spring and summer evenings the scent of hawthorn blossom, of new-mown hay, homely farmyard smells, cottage lights winking in the dust, greet and refresh the tired mind of the traveller from London.

(Macmanus, E., *Matron of Guy's*. Andrew Melrose: London, 1936.)

Others have been drawn to this extremely quiet and beautiful place with small folded hills of granite, ancient meadows of wild flowers, small inlets and protection from any marauding storm.

The sculptor Oisín Kelly had enough money from his commissions to enable him, in 1956, to fulfil a lifelong ambition: to buy a cottage in the west of Ireland. He had no previous family or other links with Co. Mayo, but was on friendly terms with Grattan and Madeleine Freyer, who ran Terrybaun Pottery near Pontoon. The Freyers heard that a cottage in Upper Massbrook, with a magnificent view across Levalley Lough, towards Nephin Mountain, was for sale, and put him in touch with the owner. The cottage was in such a remote location that the area was nicknamed 'Canada'.

Oisín went to Massbrook whenever he had holidays from school. He derived huge enjoyment from restoring the cottage and visiting neighbours in the evenings. He formed a lasting friendship with Annie and John Maloney and their family. Although he did not engage in much artistic work while staying at the cottage, he did fill many notebooks with sketches which he completed later. For example, the mountain opposite, Massbrock, inspired his 'Cloud on Nephin', which he cast in bronze in 1969, and a nearby stream gave him the idea for his 'Mountain Stream' in copper wire. His bronze 'Turf-Cutter' no doubt owes something to his own experience with a loy on his turf-bank at Massbrook. He also regularly decorated plates for Terrybaun pottery.

Grattan and Madeleine Freyer established their studio in 1984. It consists of a few cottages on hilly farmland. Now it is occupied by the Freyers' nephew Henri Hedou, and his wife Fiona.

We continue along the road, with the lake on the right-hand side. We move towards Lahardaun. Before we reach Crossmolina we take a side road down to Errew Abbey.

Errew Abbey

Errew Abbey is situated on a peninsula stretching into Lough Conn, and was founded by St Tiernan in the seventh century. It is believed that the abbey was built by the Barretts for the Augustinians on the site of an earlier church.

There is a strange story about a relic associated with this abbey: it is said that the Mias Tighernain, or the dish of Tighernain, belonged to the original founder of the abbey. Later, the O'Flynn family, the stewards of the churchlands of Errew, came into the possession of the relic. The relic was described as a large plate made of several thin pieces of copper riveted together at the edges. Centuries later, in difficult times, in return for some provisions, a member of the O'Flynn family pledged it to a Mr Knox of Rappa Castle and never recovered it. The dish came to be used by Knox's tenants for the purpose of taking oaths before the establishment of the police. It became customary to ask people to swear on the dish and believed that if they swore a false oath they would become blind in one eye.

Sometime between 1822 and 1824, Dean Lyons found people still swearing on the dish and confiscated it. After Mr Knox's death, the dish was auctioned in London with the rest of his plates. The story does not end there, and the relic is not an illusion – the famous reliquary was on display at the National Museum of Ireland in 2005, and this is what the museum had to say about it:

> This unique reliquary, which has been in the care of the National Museum of Ireland since 1999, has traditionally been associated with Errew near Crossmolina, Co. Mayo. It is a shallow circular dish made of copper alloy and its front is decorated with an equal-armed silver cross. Now worn through use, the arms of this cross are engraved with scrolls and mythical beasts. At the centre is a circular setting, now empty. The back is plain and there are many repairs visible, especially around the rim.
>
> The Mias was in the custody of the O'Flynn family who, from medieval times, were stewards of the church lands of Errew, near Crossmolina. In more recent times the Mias was kept at Mount Stewart, Rothesay, Isle of Bute, Scotland, before being acquired by the National Museum of Ireland in 1999. Crossmolina is situated on the River Deel. The town derived its name from the Irish – Cros Uí Maoilíona – as a result of a cross which was erected there in memory of O'Maoilíona, a member of the local ruling family. Errew Abbey was founded by St Tiernan, the patron of Crossmolina in the sixth century. The present ruins are those of a building of the twelfth century.

Crossmolina Abbey was founded in AD 1300 by a member of the deBarry family who held estates in Crossmolina around this time. Later it passed into the hands of Edmund Albanach Burke of Inniscoe. In AD 1386 forces from Sligo Castle devastated the orchards of Inniscoe and Castlehill. In 1526, O'Donnell of Tirconnell captured Crossmolina and Castlehill. In 1570, Richard Burke of Castlehill opposed the other Burkes of Tirawley in widespread revolt against English misrule. The English, led by Richard Bingham, won the battle at the Windy Gap in 1586 and brought the prisoners to an island on Lough Conn. (Donahue, T., *The History of Crossmolina*. De Búrca: Dublin, 2003.)

The town has not forgotten its long history. It has put it behind and has moved brightly into the twenty-first century, but the remnants of the past exist both in stone and place name. We return to Castlebar through the Windy Gap, or Bearna na Gaoithe, as it is called in Irish.

There is a platform here where visitors always stop to look down at the majestic scene below. Through this vent the winds blow and cry upon the heather. It was through this gap and during a terrible night of rain and lightning that the French and Irish dragged the French cannons. It seemed an impossible task, but Humbert was a guerrilla fighter by nature and he wished to use surprise tactics.

Humbert continued along the path to Castlebar. When the sun came up the next morning, he was ready to do battle. The event would be known thereafter as 'The Races of Castlebar'. At the 'vee' of the present road from Sion Hill sits a small mound of earth known as 'the Frenchman's Grave'. At the north entrance to the town the County Home once stood, and during the darkest days of the Famine people cried out in vain to gain entrance. Many died at the gates and were buried later in long graves. The former workhouse has now been razed to the ground and a new hospital marks the spot. The French, better trained in guerrilla tactics, split up and attacked from three sides. For this reason, the English army thought that three armies were engaging in battle. All ranks broke and fled to Tuam and later Athlone.

The River Deel in Crossmolina.

Castlebar to Ballinrobe and onwards

We set off for the Joyce country, which lies to the south and straddles Galway and Mayo. The Partry Mountains run with us in the distance. They are comfortably settled on the horizon, yet towards the end of this range lies Maamtrasna, and this name will always be associated with the murders that occurred there on 17 August 1882.

One moves along the road and then up and down and up and down until one comes to a crossroads and a sign that points to Ballintubber Abbey. Mass has consistently been celebrated at this abbey since the year of its foundation in 1216, and for Mayo people it's a symbol of a hope and resurrection.

It has had its years of ecclesiastical glory and its gory moments. It has been suppressed, neglected, ruined and it has risen from the ashes. Today it is a place of quietness and asylum. It lies in a small hollow of land and is clean of outline, with grey slates and pointed limestone. The graveyard beside it lies upon a small hillock and close to this lies Thóchar Pádraig. It is a quiet place of pilgrimage and retreat.

Though there are many references in the ancient annals to 1216 as the year of its foundation, the circumstances are shrouded in legend. Cathal was the natural son of King Turlough. Before he ascended the throne of his father he was in flight from the vengeance of Turlough's queen.

Local folklore tells us that during the period in which he worked in Ballintubber, he was treated with great kindness. Leaving Ballintubber, Cathal vowed that he would never forget the kindness shown him there by a man called Sheridan. Years afterwards, when Cathal inherited his father's throne, he visited an old friend in Ballintubber. The king asked Sheridan if he could do anything for him in return for the kindness shown him in the days of exile. Sheridan told him that he was now old and that he wanted for little in this world, but if the king would restore their old church which was collapsing, he

Ballintubber Abbey.

would be eternally grateful. Cathal went one better and promised that instead of repairing the old church he would build a new one.

Let us put the abbey in a wider historical context. Frederick II was king of Germany and Sicily between 1212 and 1250. The Magna Carta was signed in 1215. The Dominican order was founded between 1225 and 1274. During this century Aquinas and others brought the thinking of Greek philosophers to the defence of theology. It was a time infused with great intellectual enthusiasm, all over Europe. Gothic architecture flourished between 1200 and 1400. If ever we could say that architecture successfully expressed spiritual ideals, it would be in the towering Gothic structures of medieval Europe and Great Britain. Its innovative engineering and style was a testament to human ingenuity. Before that, Romanesque architecture had held sway. Now Ballintubber carries both styles. In part it is Romanesque. It is solid and firm, but then its Gothic builders introduced the dramatic technique of ribbed vaulting. It has a lightness and elegance that Roman architecture lacked. In this sense Ballintubber is an architecture that marks the ending of one system or architecture and the introduction of another.

There had been an old Celtic church where Ballintubber now stands before the present structure, which is Norman in style. It marks the end of the Irish church system and the imposition of the European church. It has withstood repression, fire, Cromwellian destruction and the grim Penal Laws, and has risen to become a beacon of spiritual light in the landscape. It has been restored and the finest of artists have contributed, with the Stations of the Cross by Imogene Stuart, stained glass by Gabriel Loire, and a wooden statue of the Virgin and Child by Oisín Kelly. More recently a bronze statue by Brother Joseph McNally was erected just within the wall. It is a spectacular piece of work, full of significance and refinement. He was a man of great spiritual depth and he was an educator of the finest quality who was born in Ballintubber, became a De La Salle Brother, and worked for most of his life in the east.

There are many glories connected to this abbey. It is a living, religious place, intense in its spirituality, mystical in its attitude. It has the atmosphere that we associate with a simpler Celtic church. It is a serious place of retreat for the spiritual wanderer and seeker.

We leave the abbey, turn left, turn left and then turn left again and we are on the road to Partry.

Partry

Partry House was built by Arthur Lynch in 1667 on the remains of Cloonlagheen Castle, as a dowager house for his mother, Lady Ellis, widow of Sir Roebuck Lynch of Castle Carra.

Sir Roebuck's lands were seized by the Cromwellians, and he was given lands at Castle Carra during the first half of the seventeenth century as compensation. The castle was named after Cloonlagheen townland, on which it stands. Evidence of the original castle was discovered during restoration work in 1995. The old castle walls are still visible as they have been incorporated into the stable walls.

At Partry we take a detour to the right. The road sign directs us towards Tourmakeady. This is an Irish-speaking district and is situated above Lough Mask and its many islands. The lake runs south into Galway. Running high above are the Partry Mountains. There is a roofless church here and it is in this graveyard that Thomas Plunkett, the Irish bishop of Tuam, is buried. George Henry Moore, the owner of Moore Hall, sold some land to the Plunketts and they built a sandstone lodge there. Later the Plunketts purchased more land from George Moore and began to proselytise the area. Because some children refused to attend the Protestant school, they were evicted.

Father Lavelle, who was a fiery-minded priest, carried out a campaign against Bishop Plunkett. It turned into a vicious international legal affair. The struggle between the two men became known as 'the War in Partry'. The biggest evictions in the area under Plunkett happened in November 1860, when large numbers of police, together with a company of troops from the Curragh, came into the area. Under the command of the Mayo High Sheriff, Colonel Knox, the brigade cleared the villages of Gortfree and Gurteenmore of their tenants in three days. These became known as the Glensaul evictions.

The Partry Mountains on the horizon: in the middle-ground the waters of Lough Carra.

The evictions were condemned in the newspapers. By 1863, Plunkett had had enough of the campaign and sold his estate to an English industrialist, Mr Mitchell, and he moved to Tuam. This era was to be followed by a period of relative calm.

There is a parallel history to this area, with its woods and great waterfall splashing down in white silken strands. They say that the sweetest Irish is spoken in Tourmakeady. An Irish summer school was founded here in 1905. To this school came the great Irish scholars of the time. They say that Douglas Hyde, who visited here, was the man who single-handedly saved the Irish language from extinction. He wrote in Irish, published many translations from Irish, was one of the founders of the Gaelic League, and President of Ireland from 1938 until 1945. He was greatly loved and created some of his finest collections of Irish poems in Mayo. He rediscovered a blind Mayo poet named Raftery, and lifted him out of the obscurity into which he had fallen. Pádraig Pearse and Éamon De Valera often visited the school, and it was here that De Valera met his wife, Sinéad Flanagan. Kuno Meyer was attracted to the area. He was professor of Celtic literature at the University of Berlin. He founded the Dublin School of Irish Learning and edited and translated many Gaelic manuscripts.

There is much more to be said of Tourmakeady but we will move up into the hills. We have reached Maamtrasna. In this bleak and remote place gruesome murders took place. The tragic events that followed are still remembered and the jury is still out on the verdict. Were the wrong people executed? The definitive book on the matter, *Maamtrasna: The Murders and The Mystery*, was written by Jarlath Waldron.

The murders were committed on 17 August 1882. Five members of one family were killed: John Joyce of Maamtrasna, his wife, his daughter, his son and his mother, along with another young boy who was left for dead with terrible injuries. A pair of brothers from the area were feuding with their cousins at the time and went to the police to give their oath, stating that they had seen their cousins going to the victim's house that night. As a result ten men were taken into custody.

As the day of the trial approached, two of the prisoners agreed to give the same evidence as the informers, even though they knew it was false. The first three prisoners, Pat Joyce, Pat Casey and Myles Joyce, were tried, found guilty and sentenced to be hanged. A priest from Clonbur successfully persuaded the remaining five to plead guilty and avoid being hanged.

Myles Joyce, Pat Joyce and Pat Casey were hanged in Galway jail on 15 December 1882. Myles Joyce had loudly proclaimed his innocence until the end; the other two even admitted that Myles had not been there the night of the murders. He was hanged regardless of this.

Of the five men that went to jail only one, Michael Casey, was guilty of the crime. Casey admitted soon after they were jailed that the four others had not been present on the night of the murder. Despite this admission, the authorities refused to release the innocent men.

The truth emerged in August 1884, when Tom Casey of Glensaul, who had given false evidence to avoid imprisonment, made an open confession to the people in Tourmakeady church. He confessed before the bishop and the congregation that he had sworn falsely and brought about the terrible miscarriage of justice.

Soon afterwards, Archbiskop McEvilly urged the government to re-open the case. The cause was taken up by Tim Harrington MP and by Parnell. The Irish Party fought long and hard in the British Parliament to free the innocent men. Eventually, the government in England fell. One of the main reasons for this was refusal to look again at the Maamtrasna case. It is the darkest of stories. The young injured child survived and was to return years later to Maamtrasna but had no recollection of what had happened.

Ballinrobe

This town is situated on the River Robe, from which it derives its name, and on the road from Hollymount to Cong; it consists of one principal street, from which two others diverge, and, in 1831, contained 441 houses, of which nearly all are well built and slated, and several are of handsome appearance. There are barracks for cavalry and infantry ... A considerable trade is carried on in corn; and large quantities of wheat and potatoes, the latter of excellent quality, are sold in the town. There is a large flour-mill, and extensive brewery and malting establishment and a tan yard, all in full operation.

(Lewis, S., *Topographical Dictionary of Mayo*. Kennikat Press: New York, 1970.).

Even in the middle of the nineteenth century Ballinrobe was a busy place and life was good. It was later in this century that George Moore would capture this world in *A Drama in Muslin*.

There are a number of ruins in the immediate vicinity of Ballinrobe. While they are not as numerous as they are to the north, east and south, there are sufficient remnants of fulachta fiadh, standing stones, enclosures, and stone circles to indicate that the area was inhabited in ancient times.

There were several abbeys in the area around Ballinrobe, including Ballintubber Abbey and Burriscarra Abbey several miles north of Ballinrobe, Inismaine Abbey on the shores of Lough Mask a few miles south-west of Ballinrobe, and Cong Abbey (in ruins), to the south of Ballinrobe. All of these abbeys have roots dating back to the sixth and seventh centuries, even if they were later enlarged and rebuilt. In the 1400s the Knights Hospitallers had a house and chapel near the abbey in Ballinrobe.

The Plague of 1348-1349, fires, plunder, and anti-Catholic laws, such as the one passed in Dublin in 1536 for the dissolution of the monasteries, all contributed to the decline of these monasteries. While the abbey in Ballinrobe

On the banks of the Ballinrobe canal.

survived later than most (Mass was celebrated in the abbey as late as 1692) by the end of the seventeenth century Ballinrobe Abbey was deserted.

Powerful Protestant English landlords took over much of southern Mayo in the early seventeenth century. The earliest landlords under the English Plantation System were the Nolans, who were Catholic, and the Cuffs, who were Protestant but reportedly more tolerant than other landlords. Many of the smaller landlords who had been Catholic switched to Protestantism in order to retain their land during the cruellest days of the Penal Laws.

It is only local descriptions that convey to the reader the dreadful scenes of the Great Famine. In the years prior to the famine, Ballinrobe workhouse could cope with the inmates who sought refuge here. With the pressure of disease and hunger, however they could not deal with the situation at the workhouse in 1847.

Dating back to 1390, Ballinrobe is said to be the oldest town in South Mayo. The registry of the Dominican friary of Athenry contains a mention to the monastery de Roba, an Augustinian friary whose recently restored ruins are one of the historical landmarks of the town today. The District Courtroom is housed in the old Market House, a marketing centre for local produce established in 1752. In 1839 the Union Workhouse of the Poor Law Union of Ballinrobe was founded. And as with other law unions of Ireland, Ballinrobe suffered greatly during the Great Famine of 1845 to 1849. With 2,000 inmates at the height of the famine, the Workhouse was so overcrowded that on 23 March 1847, the *Mayo Constitution* reported:

In Ballinrobe the workhouse is in the most awfully deplorable state, pestilence having attacked paupers, officers, and all. In fact, this building is one horrible

1. A sacred mountain, Croagh Patrick.

2. Moore Hall, a great literary house.

3. Callow Lake in late December, between Swinford and Foxford.

4. Promontory cliffs, North Mayo.

5. Lough Lannagh, seen from the woods outside Castlebar.

6. Carrowbeg River in Westport.

7. The road to the Céide fields.

8. Doolough, meaning 'Black Lake'.

9. Monument to the 1798 Rebellion at Castlebar.

10. Delphi Lodge, world-renowned fishing lodge.

11. The islands of Clew Bay.

12. Murrisk Abbey. Here begins the pilgrimage to the summit of the Reek.

13. The Moy in spate, at Foxford woollen mills.

14. Bronze figure of Michael Davitt,
Mayo's most famous son.

15. Turlough round tower, one of six in
Mayo.

16. Mayo Abbey, the site of a great Patrician foundation.

17. Round tower at Balla.

18. Achill Reservoir.

19. A small wood close to the Heinrich Böll centre.

20. Leenane, before the destruction of the bridge on Wednesday 18 July, 2007.

21. Leenane, after the flood. (Photograph © Joe O'Shaughnessy, 2007)

22. The view from Céide Fields.

23. The most westerly mosque in Europe.

24. The famous dance hall at Roheen.

25. The dominant presence of Sliabh Mór, at Achill.

26. That granite sheep may safely graze…

Charnel house, the unfortunate paupers being nearly all the victims of a fearful fever, the dying and the dead, we might say, huddled together. The master has become the victim of this dread disease; the clerks, a young man whose energies were devoted to the well-being of the union, has been added to the victims; the matron, too, is dead; and the respected, and esteemed physician has fallen before the ravages of pestilence, in his constant attendance on the diseased inmates. This is the position of the Ballinrobe house, every officer swept away, while the number of deaths among the inmates is unknown; and we forgot to add that the Roman Catholic chaplain is also dangerously ill of the same epidemic. Now the Ballinrobe board have complied with the Commissioner's orders, in admitting a houseful of paupers and in striking a new rate, which cannot be collected; while the unfortunate inmates, if they escape the awful epidemic, will survive only to be the subjects of a lingering death by starvation!

Ninety-six people died in just one week in April of 1849. The dead were buried in unmarked, shallow graves, located just outside the boundary on the southwest of the ruins. In 1922, during the Irish Civil War, a great deal of the structure was burned, although some portions remain to this day.

What really brought Ballinrobe into the limelight was Charles Cunningham Boycott. Captain Boycott was not the worst of men by any means. His nature and his background were held against him, and he never understood the Irish temperament very well. He happened to be in the wrong place at the wrong time.

A stone hen picking stone seeds in Ballinrobe.

It all began when the tenants demanded a reduction of 25 per cent on their rents. He offered a 10 per cent reduction on instructions from Lord Erne of Crom Castle, who was at this time both old and senile and lived far away far from the problem. Boycott served eviction notices against eleven of his tenants. On 22 September David Sears, accompanied by seventeen constables, set off from Ballinrobe to serve notices. The women of the Lough Mask area descended on them with mud, stones and manure. They took shelter in Lough Mask House.

The following day they tried again to serve the notices. Suddenly a swell of people rushed from Ballinrobe along the road to Lough Mask House. The move had been inspired by the genial parish priest of the Neale, John O'Malley, and by James Redpath, the special correspondent of the *New York Herald* who had thrown his sympathies in with the Land League and was the man who first brought the word 'boycott' into circulation. The people swarmed across the estate, invaded the house and advised the servants to abandon their posts. On 23 September Captain and Mrs Boycott, their niece and nephew, and Ashton Weekes found themselves isolated at Lough Mask House.

Within a few days the blacksmith refused to shoe the captain's horses and the laundress refused to do the washing. The twelve-year-old post boy refused to carry letters from Ballinrobe and shopkeepers refused to serve them food and other necessities. By early October the Boycotts were isolated. On 28 September a hut had been sent to Lough Mask House to shelter the police who had been brought in to protect the estate. All this drew only local attention.

At Lough Mask House, Captain Boycott now found himself rising at four in the morning to feed the cattle and milk the cows, while his wife learned to cook and clean for herself. He wondered would he ever harvest his root crops, which were worth £500. The events were talked about locally but the papers, even the local ones, had not picked up the story. But already, by 23 September, the word 'boycott' had found its way into circulation. John Redpath maintained that while he was dining with Fr O'Malley they had searched around for a word to describe what had happened. They tested several phrases and words: 'social excommunication' and 'ostracism' they found too difficult. 'No,' said Fr O'Malley, 'ostracism wouldn't do.' He looked down for a moment, tapped his forehead, and said, 'How would it do to call it "to Boycott him"?' They had struck on the word in the Neale Presbytery over dinner.

By 11 October Captain Boycott called for extra police protection and sought help from the RIC to carry his mail. On 18 October *The Times* carried a letter which he had sent to them, with an editorial comment.

It was at this point that Bernard Becker of the *London Daily News* entered the story. He had come in search of news, working between Castlebar, Claremorris and Westport. He had read Boycott's letter in *The Times* but when he reached Claremorris nobody wished to talk about the gentleman and there was total silence when he mentioned the name at Ballinrobe. He headed for Lough Mask House. The constables refused him entry so he wandered about the perimeter of the estate. As he rounded a bend, there in front of him stood Captain Boycott with his wife, trying to herd some sheep. The captain gave him one of the longest interviews he was to give to anybody, as he was a man of few words. Becker immediately sat down to write a human interest story, under the title, 'The isolation of Captain Boycott', and dispatched it to his paper. He was a clear writer and he gave both sides of the story. The article was reprinted in the *Belfast Newsletter* and the *Dublin Express*. A Mr Manning in Dublin then proposed the idea of salvaging Captain Boycott's crops. The *Belfast Newsletter* later established a Boycott relief fund. Money began to flow into the fund and sympathy for Captain Boycott began to grow. The next idea to take root was that of an Ulster expedition to Mayo. Labourers came forward as volunteers. A large body of men came to Mayo by train to save the crops. The organisers of the expedition demanded military protection for the escort and so more people got involved.

On 1 November Captain Boycott had to attend the petty sessions in Ballinrobe. As he left the court he was surrounded by a hostile crowd of some 500. He took shelter in the infantry barracks. He was brought home with a large escort. Mr McSheehy, the resident magistrate, wrote to Dublin on 3 November for more infantry. The government wished to house these men in the workhouse, but the Board of Guardians refused them permission. The government, in the meantime, made it clear that it would not permit an invasion of Ulstermen, so in the north they settled on sending a contingent of men from Monaghan and Cavan. On 9 November extra troops from Dublin were ordered into Mayo. At the Broadstone terminus in Dublin, wagons were hitched, horses loaded into boxes, ambulances strapped down, gear checked, food supplies stored, and then at the break of dawn they were all on their way. In the meantime the Curragh was full of activity. Four hundred soldiers, with officers and gear, were dispatched to Mayo through Athlone.

On Wednesday 10 November the weather was foul at Claremorris. The soldiers, cold and hungry, awaited their marching orders to Ballinrobe which was thirteen miles away, wondered what the whole exercise was about. They finally reached Ballinrobe and pitched tents on the green between the infantry and cavalry barracks. Soon the green was a quagmire. By the end of that day there were 1,000 wet and miserable troops in Ballinrobe and with them were the reporters. They came from Britain and America to cover the largest invasion of Mayo since that of General Humbert. And rumours circulated among the people. Two thousand Ulstermen were on the way into Mayo. This surely augured trouble. There were reports of old Enfield guns and revolvers in the hands of the young men of the area. For Captain Boycott, things were getting out of control. Fifteen men would have saved his crops and now fifty labourers were coming from Ulster. He did not have the means to feed such a number. One hundred infantry men had already pitched camp on his estate.

At Mullingar on Thursday 11 November, contingents from Cavan and Monaghan converged. At Athlone station the fifty were given revolvers. From Athlone to Claremorris, they were hissed and booed at as they passed through the stations, while a special engine went ahead to make sure there was no interference from the Land Leaguers.

At two o'clock in the afternoon, Claremorris station was sealed off by Hussars and Dragoons and infantrymen. James Daly of the *Connaught Telegraph* was on the platform and he whiled away the time with a denunciation of landlordism. At three o'clock they arrived. Bayonets were fixed and orders issued to fire if an Ulsterman was attacked. Then the volunteers emerged from the train, weary and wondering. James Daly told them to be of good cheer, and that nobody in Mayo would soil their hands with them. 'What kind of a b… is this Boycott?', one of the labourers asked, and Daly told him that he wasn't worth the bother he was causing.

Up the town they started, 400 men protecting 50, fully armed, ready for any eventuality. It was almost dark now, and the rain was heavy and perpetual. It fell in sheets upon them, and they cursed at the awful Mayo weather and splashed on through the pools of water. Five hours later they reached Ballinrobe. The streets were lined with infantrymen, and behind them the people were booing and jeering. The labourers made for the infantry barracks tired and weary, and this was only the end of the first day.

Friday 12 November dawned. The weather was no different and the ground was still sodden. Under heavy escort they set out for Lough Mask House. There were only a few women and children on the road as they passed along. They sang Land League songs and told them, 'hurry up, the turnips is boiling'.

When they finally reached Lough Mask House there was a set-to between the contingents regarding who would have the better tent. Finally they settled on tents towards central poles. Outside it was one of the worst nights of the year, with rain and high winds. The next morning they set about their task, which was to harvest two acres of potatoes, eight acres of turnips, seven acres of mangolds and twenty acres of corn. They worked surrounded by police and soldiers. And all this was followed by the eyes of the world. Much to the disappointment of the reporters no hard news broke. Nothing was happening except that the harvest was going ahead at a great cost, for Parnell reckoned it cost a shilling to lift each turnip.

By Wednesday, while the world looked on and newsmen searched for some story or other, the potatoes and mangolds had been harvested. And on the same day Captain Boycott admitted to the heavy strain that events were imposing both on himself and his wife Annie. He wished to leave the place.

The first week ended. There had been no bloodshed. The weather had been wretched and the troops were uncomfortable. The word boycott had entered the English dictionary. The eyes of the world were upon Ballinrobe and the Irish situation.

On Saturday 20 November, Boycott's cattle, under escort, were sent to Claremorris station. People booed and hissed them as they passed by. The animals finally reached Dublin but the drovers refused to touch them. They were sold at a good price privately.

On the farm itself, work went ahead. Hay from Kilmaine was brought to the estate under heavy escort and the threshing continued. On 23 November the newly-threshed corn was carried to Dublin through Cong. By 25 November the workers had almost finished the harvesting and Mr Wynne visited the area and recorded the scene for posterity. Fr John O'Malley was busy placarding the area with instructions to let the Orangemen and the English army depart from the area without bother. People's attitudes towards the labourers softened and it was said the some of them had become Land Leaguers once they had really understood the situation.

On Friday 26 November the expedition prepared to leave. That night the worst storm ever recorded broke over the area and it was said that the weather had entered the services of the Land League. The telegraph wires were down and the correspondents could not get their stories through.

On Saturday at two o'clock in the afternoon they prepared for their departure. The camps were taken down, bundled up and put on wagons, and the waterlogged ground was covered with boxes and canisters. They all gathered in front of the house to say goodbye to Captain Boycott and his lady. The captain, moving among them, shook hands and seemed moved by emotion. Then they marched out through the gates and on to Ballinrobe under a clear sky. There were few on the road to watch them. They stayed the night in Ballinrobe and the next day set off on their journey home. They were passed on the road by Captain Boycott, his wife and his nieces, in an ambulance wagon which they had to borrow. The family departed quietly from Claremorris station. Later the labourers departed on another train. They travelled to Athlone without incident and there the men of the 184th Regiment said goodbye to the Ulstermen and proceeded to the Curragh.

Captain Boycott stayed in the Hamman Hotel in Dublin but had to leave when the proprietor received warning letters. He left for England on 1 December.

And so the story more or less ends. He returned to Lough Mask House a year later without undue fuss and no hostility was shown towards him. In February 1886, he returned to England to sell his lease at Lough Mask and he had the added bonus of £2,000, which he received from public subscription. He often returned to his Kildarra estate nearby and spent his holidays there. In England he became secretary to a local race committee and he continued to have a great interest in horses. And that is how the word 'boycott' was introduced to the English language.

Back to our journey: at the square, or triangle, you turn left and make your way to Cong, the burial place of the last High King of Ireland. Cong is known the world over because John Ford, the American director, decided to make a film here. *The Quiet Man* was a magical moment for Ireland and Cong. For the first time, the Irish in America saw the beauty of Ireland in Technicolor. The lands of which their grandparents spoke opened before them. It was a film that was made joyously and this was obvious in the work itself. The producers were none too pleased to be making a 'cowboy' film in Ireland, but when the rough cuts were studied in Hollywood, they knew they had a hit on their hands. They did not realise that they had created a classic.

The ancient abbey of Cong is set close to running water and mature trees. It is built on an ancient site, for St Fechin founded a small monastery there in the seventh century and Turlough O'Connor, King of Connaught built a monastery in 1120 for the Augustinians. It attracted some 3,000 students in its great day and the last king of Ireland, Rory O'Connor, spent the last twelve years of his life there.

The ancient cloisters at Cong Abbey.

The large processional cross called the Cross of Cong is one of the wonders of its age. It is now preserved in the National Museum. It was created in the twelfth century under the patronage of Turlough O'Connor and is regarded as one of the finest examples of a processional cross of its time. The Bachall Buí, or yellow crozier, was made in Roscommon in 1123 from gold mined at Croagh Patrick. It is made of oak and stands thirty inches high with arm extent measuring nineteen inches. It is covered with silver and bronze plates, washed with gold. Its edges were studded with precious stones and a large crystal in the centre covered the relic enshrined in the cross. The cross is so richly decorated with carved animal heads and intricate interlacing, that even the nail heads that are used are shaped like animal heads.

The cross was guarded by the Augustinians of Cong and was placed on the altar only on very special occasions. With the sixteenth century came persecution and hardship to the religious orders in Ireland and the Augustinians were forced to leave Cong. One abbot remained as the parish priest until his death in 1829. His successor, on taking over the abbot's house, found several treasures hidden within. The Bachall Buí was among them.

Everyone is familiar with Ashford Castle from the opening scene in *The Quiet Man*. Ashford Castle was built in 1228 on the banks of Lough Corrib by the Anglo-Norman De Burgo family. Following generations added and expanded the castle, and in 1715 the Oranmore and Browne family founded the Ashford Estate. Over 100 years later, in 1852, Sir Benjamin Lee Guinness purchased the Ashford Estate. His son Lord Ardilaun inherited Ashford in 1868 and is responsible for the numerous woodland areas on the estate. He is fondly remembered in Cong. After withdrawing from the Guinness Company in 1876, Sir Arthur Guinness was created Baron Ardilaun of Ashford, in the County of Galway in 1880. His title derived from the Gaelic 'Ard Oileán', meaning a 'high island' on the lake.

Oscar Wilde's father and mother were frequent visitors to this area. Oscar's father, Sir William Wilde, was multi-talented. He was, amongst other things, an outstanding surgeon and an antiquarian. I take the following from his book *Wilde's Lough Corrib*:

Left: Entrance to Ashford Castle.

Below: Ashford Castle.

Continuing our route on to the village of Cong, through the great cairn-studded plain of Moytura, we meet another small ancient church called Cillársa, in the townland of Ballymagibbon, of which twelve feet high of the east gable, with a small, round arched window in it, still remains. Again, a little nearer the lake, in the village of Gort a' Churra, 'the field of the currach' (scrub or bottom), there formerly existed the ruins of a very small church, some of the large stones of which may still be discerned in the adjoining walls and cottages.

From the hill of Tonlegee, overlooking this latter locality, was taken the accompanying view of Moytura House, the residence of the Author, erected in 1865; and so-called after the ancient battlefield on which it stands, with Benlevi Mountain in the distance, and Loch Corrib in front. The tower with the flagstaff stands within the enclosure of one of the ancient cathairs of the battlefield. This house commands a magnificent prospect to the west, south, and east, and can be seen from most parts of the middle lake. To the west of Moytura is Leaca Fionna – 'white flagstones' – the residence of Ormsby Elwood, Esq.; and still nearer to Cong, over a small bay of the lake, stands Lios Luachra – 'the rushy liss', or earthen fort – the residence of William Burke, Esq.

We have passed the last navigation mark, and laid our course nearly due north towards the Cong River. From this point the mountain view presents one of its best aspects, and the shores of Mayo and Galway, sloping down to the water's edge, are in many places pleasingly wooded. Leaving Coad Island on the left, we get among a group of islets at the mouth of the river, the outermost of which, Oileán na Rí, or 'the king's island,' was said to have been a favourite retreat of O'Conor, the last Irish monarch, while sojourning in the neighbouring abbey; and nearer the shore are Inis Cunga and Oileán Dara.

Now, dividing the waters of Mayo and Galway, we pass Ceann a' Doire, 'the head of the oak wood', and enter the principal stream way which conducts the waters of Loch Mask into Loch Coirib. Well sheltered, wooded on both sides, having Kinlough on the right, the demesne of Ashford on the left, and Strandhill, the sea of the Elwoods, in front, with the pretty spire of the parish church in the distance, it forms a picture of great beauty. The following illustration, taken from the eastern shore, represents the 'Eglinton' passing under the demesne of Ashford, the noble seat of Sir B. L. Guinness, MP, with its tower rising over the surrounding woods.

(Wilde, W., *Wilde's Lough Corrib*. Duffy, 2002.)

This passage may be slightly pompous but it demonstrates William Wilde's interest in landscape and the meaning of place names.

Shrule is the final town on the southern edge of Mayo. A tower built for the defence of the bridge against marauding enemies lies close to the Black River. This strong construction was erected in around 1238, and had a peaceful history until 1570, when it was captured by Sir Edward Fitton and a strong British force. The massacre of Shrule, in 1641, makes for grim reading.

When the great insurrection civil war broke out in October 1641, the English Protestant settlers of North Mayo fled for safety to the castles of some of the important men in the county. One of these refugees was the Protestant Bishop of Killala, Dr John Maxwell. With his wife, his three children and some servants, he first fled from Killala to Sir Henry Bingham's castle at Castlebar, but Sir Bingham surrendered that castle to Myles Burke, Second Lord Viscount Mayo, who had joined the rebellious Irish. Lord Mayo brought the English refugees to his own castle in Belcarra, where he sheltered and protected them for some time. He then made arrangements to escort them to Shrule and there deliver them to another escort from Co. Galway. Accordingly, on 9 February 1642, he, his eldest son Sir Theobald Burke, and about 100 soldiers, escorted the refugees toward Shrule. They arrived on the evening of 12 February.

The next day, Lord Mayo sent home four of the five groups of soldiers and gave the Maxwell family over to the custody of the remaining company of soldiers commanded by one Edmund Burke, brother of Walter Burke of Cloghan in Kilmaine, with orders to bring them to Kilnemannagh in Co. Galway, where the Galway escort was to meet them. Lord Mayo directed his son to accompany the escort, the refugees, with horses. He then took off with a few men for Cong to shelter from the weather. No sooner had he left than Edmund Burke and the escort fell upon the refugees. Dr Maxwell and his wife were stripped naked and the bishop was wounded by a blow to the head. Lord Mayo's son tried to stop the massacre but the soldiers threatened him, and would have killed him if it hadn't been for John Garvey of Lehinch, the captain of the escort, who dragged him by the arm, carried him over the bridge and put him on a horse, making him ride away.

The massacre continued for three hours, until Ulick Burke of Castle Hacket and the friars of Ross Abbey arrived with help to rescue the survivors. Around forty men survived. Dr Maxwell and his family stayed at Castle Hacket and were seen by a doctor, while the others were lodged in houses around Headford and cared for by the friars. Lord Clanrickard sent a large escort to bring the bishop and his family to Galway and they were eventually taken by boat to Dublin.

Shrule is peaceful now. The castle is empty and it stands a little off the roadway surrounded by a few trees. The land about is fertile and well parcelled out and defined by straight limestone walls. We have reached the borders of Mayo and it is time to return to Castlebar by way of Moore Hall and Carnacon.

Kilmaine, Hollymount

Kilmaine belongs to that area in Mayo where the land is good, the grass sweet and memories are retained within prehistoric remains: ring forts, standing stones, and ancient dolmens and many other marks left by the earliest inhabitants of the area.

It is desirable land and that is why the Normans took possession of it. The Normans spread across the country from the south-east and the east. The Anglo-Norman colonisation of Ireland began in 1169 and Mayo came under Norman control in 1235. Ireland saw the eclipse of the lords and chieftains. The great Celtic family of the O'Connors of Connaught was supplanted by newcomers. The invaders soon adopted Gaelic customs and began to marry with the native Irish. Examples of Mayo surnames still in existence today, with Norman origins include: Barrett, Burke and Bourke, Costello, Culkin, Davitt, Fitzmaurice, Gibbons, Jennings, Joyce, McEvilly, Nally, Padden, Staunton and Walsh. The Normans brought continental order with them, as well as a Gothic style of building and organisation. The Normans started numerous towns and developed some existing settlements into towns, as well as organising fairs and markets. They developed roads, bridges and sea ports, and promoted the growth of trade, both domestic and foreign, as well as improving the agricultural methods then in vogue.

The Normans of course set up a whole empire. In their time it stretched down to Sicily, across the Mediterranean to the Holy Land. Like all empires, it eventually ran out of steam. A great battle took place in Athenry in Co. Galway. The Second Battle of Athenry took place on 10 August 1316 and was one of the most decisive battles in the province for the Normans. The battle apparently took place on the boggy plain to the east of the town, outside the tower gate called the Laragh Gate. Twenty-three-year-old King Felim was one of the many casualties. The Second Battle of Athenry marked the definitive end of the power of the O'Connors as kings of Connaught.

The annals tell us that Kilmaine was burned by Manus O'Connor and Milo de Cogan in 1177. In 1595, Red Hugh O'Donnell had held a great assembly here.

On 21 January 1747, Robert Miller of Milford was fatally wounded in a duel with John Browne near Kilmaine and died a few days later. John Browne was from the Neale. He wished to become a member of 'The True Blue Club of Kilmaine'. One of the rules of the club was that anyone who had a Catholic grandfather could not be admitted. John Browne was refused on this account by Robert Miller, who was president at the time. John Browne objected to the refusal and wrote a letter to Miller. Miller immediately replied that the prohibition was not meant as a personal affront to Browne or anyone else but was merely a way of preventing the club from growing too big. James French, who had carried the letter, had instructions from Browne to open Miller's reply and if it was not a favourable one to inform Miller that Browne would meet him at two o'clock that day, beside the turlough near George Blake's castle in Killernan

Browne was accompanied to the field by friends from the Neale. They carried weapons and were ready for action. Before the duel there was an attempt to heal the row but to no avail. Browne carried his own pistol and slugs that he had melted from lead. They had two shots each. Browne wheeled about and shot Miller. Miller returned fire but with his second shot Browne dealt Miller a deadly blow from which he did not recover. It later came to light that Browne had loaded his pistol with illegal slugs. Browne wrote a number of letters to Robert Lindsay in the day that followed expressing his regret for what had happened and his hope for Miller's recovery. Miller survived for a few days but died on Tuesday 26 January.

The verdict rendered by the coroner was that of deliberate murder. Browne was convicted and became an outlaw. He surrendered later and a trial took place in Dublin. John Browne died in October in 1762. The quiet village of Kilmaine has had a surprisingly turbulent history.

We take the road to Hollymount. The great ballad singer Delia Murphy is associated with this area. She was our greatest balladeer and her voice has been heard all around the world. She made the Irish ballad respectable and she influenced generations of ballad singers who were to follow. Her voice could carry all the emotions from the quiet and haunting 'The Castle Of Dramore', to the delightful and romantic 'If I were a Blackbird' and many others. After a long and interesting life she died in 1971 and is buried in Deansgrange cemetery, Dublin, beside her husband, Dr T.J. Kiernan.

Hollymount.

Her biographer Aidan O'Hara met her on a hot, humid day in Ontario in August 1968. Most people in Ireland at the time probably thought she was dead:

She was farming 'way out in the sticks', as people said. She was very informal when they met and said, 'Sure, I'm from Mayo, God help us, where the crows ate the man.' But then later her mood turned and she said, 'I must have been thinking about my husband, Dr Tom Kiernan. He died last year, you know. And I'd like to sing this song which reminds me of him … She sang a most plaintive and moving song called 'Cold Blows the Wind'. The mood of the first meeting and the mood engendered by the song belong to two different worlds. Delia Murphy occupied many worlds in her time. Her father was Jack Murphy from near Hollymount. He emigrated, but one day, looking at Mount Jennings, he promised himself that he would one day purchase it. He followed the road to Klondike, but his money was not made there but in Colorado. He lived tough and rough and on the way he lost a finger. He met a young Irish woman named Anna Agnes Fanning and married her. They returned to Ireland and, as he promised himself, he purchased Mount Jennings house. His daughter Delia became a great friend of the Travellers. She said, 'People said I must not mix with the tinkers. But that was of no importance to me as well it wasn't. Except for me, the daughter of a well-to-do farmer, Tom Maughan was friendless at school. Such snobbery in the hearts of young children! I never shared their snobbery, then or since.'
(O'Hara, A., *I'll Live 'til I Die*. Drumlin Publications: Leitrim, 1997.)

Even as a young girl she had a free-ranging mind and compassion, and this helped her get into the heart of a song. She had a keen interest in local stories and ballads. She passed through various schools and eventually attended Galway University, where she met her husband. He was a part-time lecturer at the university. He accompanied her on the piano when she sang at parties. She was very outgoing while he was a quiet, scholarly man. He obtained his doctorate and advanced in the civil service. They lived in London, where their children were born. She met everybody of account in London and it was at middle-class parties that she developed her technique for singing. Someone from HMV was present at one such party and so impressed was he by her voice that he recorded her songs, nearly 100 in all. When these songs were broadcast on the BBC she became an instant success. Her husband was appointed Irish ambassador to the Vatican in 1941 and was there during the war. Other important ambassadorial posts were offered to her husband. He was Irish ambassador to Germany, Canada, and the United States of America. She met many famous people such as Count John McCormack, James Joyce, Rommel, Kesselring, and Mussolini, but was never impressed by anyone. Her life was tempestuous, but when she reached Canada she purchased a farm in a remote area. Aidan O'Hara described an encounter she had with James Joyce in his book:

> Among the famous people Delia claims she met in London was the writer James Joyce. She says she could never figure out *Finnegans Wake* or *Ulysses*, and so, one day, she said to Joyce, 'Now, you'll tell me about it or you'll never get out of my house.' 'So he read aloud many passages to me and suddenly shouted, "Kiernan, I've got it! You mustn't read *Ulysses* like a book. There's music in it."' According to Delia, Joyce went on to say that as you don't look for the composer's meaning in a Beethoven symphony, so you mustn't look for logic or meaning in [Joyce's] words.
> (O'Hara, A., *I'll Live 'til I Die*. Drumlin Publications: Leitrim, 1997.)

Eventually she returned to Ireland and purchased a cottage at the Strawberry Beds close to Lucan. She was four days shy of her sixty-ninth year when she died in St Kevin's Hospital. She suffered a massive heart attack. She was certainly a woman who led an extraordinary life.

Moore Hall

Through small roads we must now travel to Moore Hall. It is in ruins and rises above the forests that lie about it. It is the most famous house in Mayo. On 4 and 5 February 1923 the house was set alight. There was no reason why it should have been set on fire, for it was of no strategic importance and the reason for burning this famous and patriotic house still remains a mystery. In a letter to the novelist George Moore, James Reilly wrote:

> At five o'clock I ventured out, it was then pitch dark and pouring rain, imagine my horror, when I got to the hill overlooking the garden, and saw the whole house one seething mass of flames, huge tongues of fire were shooting out of every door and window, clouds of sparks, like snow flakes were being carried away by the wind which was S.W. ... At six o'clock the roof went in with one huge crash and there was nothing left only smouldering ruins of my favourite charge on which I have spent twelve years jealous care. It sickens me when I think of it all.
>
> (Hone, J. *The Moores of Moore Hall*. Jonathan Cape: London, 1939.)

The house, famous in each generation, did not deserve this fate. Attempts to restore it have all been half-hearted.

The story of Moore Hall begins when George Moore, who had made his fortune in the wine trade in Alicante in Spain, set his eye upon the site of his house on Muckloon Hill, running down to Lough Carra. He chose a most beautiful location, for below him lay a lake with many islands, covered with fragile woods, and in the distance stood the blue mountains of Partry.

He decided that this was the place to build his house and set out on its high parapet the following legend, '*Fortis cadere cedere non potest.*' Someone has suggested it should be translated thus: 'Scratch a Moore and your own blood will flow.'

The woods of Moore Hall.

George Moore's Lough Carra.

Thus the first Moore and his refined wife from Alicante settled here. She often sat on the balcony, looked towards the lake and thought of Spain. She was never happy here, while George Moore himself went blind and wept because he could not look at the beauty of the lake and the countryside. His son John joined the French and was made first President of Connaught by Humbert. He was later taken in chains to Waterford, where he died. Almost two centuries later his remains were brought home to Castlebar and interred in the Mall.

John's brother George was a quieter man. He was not interested in military matters. He became a philosopher instead. He married one of the Altamonts. His wife took over the running of the house and her husband settled into a sedentary life of writing. He had a huge library at his disposal and his book on the British Revolution of 1688 was published in 1817. He was a quiet, melancholic man.

George's sons George Henry and Augustus were different kettles of fish. Their lives were boisterous, and Augustus, who was a mathematician and a sportsman, died very young. His life had been full of promise. Like all the Moores he had an inordinate interest in horses. He was given to racing, hunting and horse training. Everything else seemed unimportant to him. He also studied mathematics at Cambridge and seemed to have a brilliant future ahead of him. But the horses were his undoing. He was more interested in going to the hunt, jumping dangerous fences and breeding horses in the stables to the rear of the great house than seeing to his studies. In 1845, Augustus set off for Liverpool with a horse called 'Mickey Free'. He did not return. The Liverpool course had become hardened by frost. At a jump 'Mickey Free' broke his back and Augustus was carried to the hospital. George rushed to Liverpool to be beside his brother for two nights and two days. When he died he was carried to Moorehall and buried in the family cemetery beside the lake.

George Henry Moore was a formidable figure. He was born in 1810 and was sent to St Mary's Ascot for his education. He too was greatly interested in horses. He was a good classical scholar, like his father. His youth was misspent, and he was so careless that his mother believed he would be carried home in a coffin. He was sent to London to study law but the call of the racetrack was too much for him and he fell into debt despite his allowance of £400 a year. Like all young men of the town from the great houses, he went on the continental tour, which took him, not only to the cities of Europe, but into Russia, to the Caucasus, beloved of Tolstoy. They went to Tiflis and Teheran. He went as far as the Dead Sea.

In Greece he fell in love with a woman, but she rejected him. He recalls the event with bitterness in his diary. He kept a notebook of this journey but the most interesting parts are his exact and professional pen drawings of what he saw. He sent several letters to Moore Hall concerning his visits. Maria Edgeworth, who visited Moore Hall, was very impressed by his ability. None of these letters remain. In September, his father died and he inherited Moore Hall and the other properties. The terrible famine came and by a stroke of luck no one on the Moore lands died, and all because of a horse called 'Corunna':

> A wonderful racing success came Moore's way in May, when his horse Corunna, ran in conjunction with Lord Waterford and won the Chester Cup. The race brought him £10,000, all good money ... He at once lodged £1,000 to his mother's account at Westport, directing her to use £500 according to her judgement, with the sole limitation that every one of his tenants, or squatters, should receive immediate relief, and that all work required in return should be for the improvement of their holdings; the other £500 should be given in mere charity to the poorest people about Moore Hall, whether in the form of a cow, or some article of necessary comfort. 'The horses', he told his mother, 'would gallop all the faster with the blessings of the poor.'
> (Hone, J., *The Moores of Moore Hall*. Jonathan Cape: London, 1939.)

He was elected MP for Mayo in 1847 when he supported Gavin Duffy's tenants' rights movement, which alienated him from many of his class. He lost some elections but was returned in 1868. The Mayo tenants, who he had sought to protect in his policies, suddenly refused to pay their rents. He returned to Moore Hall to look into the matter but died suddenly of a heart attack.

The funeral to Kiltoom graveyard was formal. The fiery Fr Lavelle gave the oration. It was high-flown and no mention was made of those who conspired not to pay their rents. Looking on with a caustic and perceptive eye was another George Moore. He was the new owner of Moore Hall and he made a vow that he would never do anything to deserve a popular funeral. This request was more or less fulfilled.

So much has been written about this George Moore that it has thrown the rest of the family into the background, but they were all talented people. They were academics, artists, mathematicians, writers, land owners, parliamentarians and county gentry.

George Moore set off for Paris with his batman Mullowney, who was more literate than George. George was a dapper man, a boulevardier, and he had a fine sense of style. He intended to become an artist but did not have any great ability in this field. He was fortunate, because he went to Paris during its golden years and there he met everyone who was anybody. He met Manet, Degas, Pissarro, Renoir, and Zola, to mention but a few. He realised he had little talent for painting and took to writing instead. Eventually, he published the first realistic set of short stories, *The Untilled Field*, an autobiography, *Confessions of a Young Man*, *Ester Waters*, and a vast number of other works.

Yeats did not like him. Yeats had always aspired to live in the great houses and Moore had the swagger of one who belonged in their great rooms. Moore could entertain and liked conversation. Yeats was self-centred, priest-like in attitude towards his poetry, and a bore. George died in 1933 in London and at his own request his ashes were buried on Castle Island in Lough Carra, across the lake from Moore Hall. His life overshadowed that of his brother Maurice Moore.

Maurice was a military man. He passed out of Sandhurst with honours and went to India with the Connaught Rangers. Later he was posted to Mauritius and Capetown and he saw action in the war against the Zulus. He was promoted to the rank of major and later to the rank of colonel. He settled at Moore Hall for many years and managed the estate until it was burned down during the Civil War in 1923. He resigned his commission as Brigadier in the British army after the Easter Rebellion and he helped with the appeal for the life of Casement. Later he became a much-loved senator of the new Irish state.

The ruins of Moore Hall stand sadly amidst the woods, close to the beautiful lake of Lough Carra. It is waiting to be called back into life, for it is more worthy of being restored than many another ruined house. The ghosts of the Moores will always haunt this enchanted place.

Before the Moores settled on Muckloon Hill the area had been already inhabited as far back as the Stone Age. We know this because at Doon stands a vast fortification wall which protected the peninsula from attack.

Castleburke stands on a ledge of limestone above Lough Carra. It lay in ruins for many years, until it was purchased by Éamonn de Burca, who is gradually restoring the castle and the Hanging House beside it.

Though now diminished in grandeur, much colourful history and folklore is attached to this ruin. Formerly known as Kilboynell Castle it was thought to have been built by O'Flahertys, but it is the Burke (MacWilliam) associations that distinguish it. Richard an Iárainn (Iron Dick) and Granuaile had one son, Tióboid Na Long (Theobald of the Ships). He acquired the castle and most of the land from McEvillys. He was a brilliant tactician and politician and at the Battle of Kinsale in 1601, he was rewarded with land and a title. On his way from the castle to Ballintubber he was killed by his brother-in-law. His descendants resided in Castleburke, which was frequently visited by poets and bards, the most notable of whom was O'Carolan, 'the Blind Harpist', who composed 'The Lords of Mayo' here.

It was built in the thirteenth century by Adam De Standún, an Anglo-Norman from Warwickshire who was a subject of De Burgo, the chief of Connaught. It is one of five Norman castles in this locality.

Castlebar to Belcarra and Balla to Claremorris

Belcarra is set in a gentle landscape of small hills that was fashioned this way during the Ice Age. It is called Baile na Caradh in Irish, which translates into 'the town of the Wier'. There was a castle here once, which belonged to the Burkes but that has disappeared.

Close by is Elm Hall and this was once the home of Lord Tyrawley. The cemetery here was what was known as 'a mixed graveyard', with both Catholics and Protestants being buried here. This caused controversy in the nineteenth century with the church authorities. There are stories told of Protestant burials taking place at night to avoid trouble.

Elmhall graveyard is of great archaeological and historical interest. Tumulus graves were discovered in the Carrajames area between 1934 and 1936. Bronze Age burial grounds were found, showing evidence of habitation as early as 2000 BC. My ancestors lived upon a drumlin back in Walshpool close to Belcarra. At the centre of a reedy lake, which is the source of a tributary of the Moy, stands a perfect crannóg. My mother came from a mountain village beyond this lake. From this small farm and from the mountain village my ancestors set out to find a better life in America and England.

Close also is Ballinafad House. It belonged to the Blake Family, became a college and is now a farm. George Moore, in his famous, some may say infamous, autobiography *Hail and Farewell*, writes this of a Blake relation:

Llewellyn Blake is my uncle, my mother's youngest brother, and he came into the property of Ballinafad on the death of Joe Blake, famous in the County Mayo for many racehorses and a love story. Joe seems to have been the only one in the family whose soul did not trouble him. His brother Mark, from whom he inherited the property in Ballinafad, was a fine old country rake, leaving samples of his voice and demeanour and appearance in every village,

Belcarra.

and then going to Dublin to repent his sins, attaining in the last years of his life the spectacular appearance of Father Christmas, causing much annoyance in the chapels that he frequented from his incurable habit of interrupting the services with Oh, Lord; my unfortunate soul!
(Moore, G., *Hail and Farewell*. Colin Smythe: Buckinghamshire, 1985.)

Reluctantly I leave Belcarra and set of for Manulla. There is a famous railway station here. George Moore mentions it memorably in his autobiography and many of my relations from the drumlins and the mountains left here in search of a livelihood abroad. They were part of the Irish diaspora and this station was their Wailing Wall. We turn to the right and head for beautiful Balla.

Beautiful Balla

The main street of Balla must be as wide as the Champs Elysées, and the air which blows through the town healthy and brisk.

Balla would have been a market town and as such it has attracted many people to its market square. Close to the square is a round tower. Balla is surrounded by good land. Archaeological remains that pre-date the Christian presence here have been found in the area.

Beyond the round tower is a simple ruin. There is a small and gentle stream here and a sacred well. There was a shelter for the blind and the lame here, for when they resorted to the well on Patron Day. But it is more than a shelter. It is the remains of a small church. I cannot say when it was built, but it most likely marks an ancient foundation. Perhaps this was a pagan well, for the pre-Christians worshipped waters and wells, and it was Christianised by St Patrick or by St Crónan (sometimes called Mochua). But it must have always been a place of pilgrimage. Much of Manulla's early history is dominated by St Patrick. In 440 the ancient territory of Corca Theimne was visited by Patrick during his travels in Mayo. It was in the plain of Finmagh that he visited the well of Slán: an important place of pagan worship and sacrifice. Patrick uncovered the dolmen over the well and by so doing defied the pagan god to punish him after interfering with his altar. After no harm came to Patrick he baptised thousands at the well. Hence for the next 900 years Manulla was known as Slán Patrick, retaining the name until the fourteenth century.

It is often called Our Lady's Blessed Well at Balla, and in the early nineteenth century between 15,000 and 20,000 pilgrims would be present in Balla on 15 August. The round tower once stood thirty metres high. It is associated with St Mochua.

Religiously, the whole area was active at the time. These monasteries were interconnected in a loose way and the monks were intrepid travellers. St

Pilgrim Church at Balla.

Round Tower at Balla.

Cronan was a great traveller. He knew the religious gossip of the time and would have been well aware of the work of Columcille who died on Iona around in the year St Cronan was born. He knew all that was happening on Iona and further down the coast in Lindisfarne. He was in contact with all the other saints of Mayo and knew the monks living on the islands off the coast.

Like the local chieftains, they would have built an enclosure of clay not unlike the raths and forts that dot the countryside. Within this enclosure they had their clay and wattle cells, which offered some protection from wind and rain. Some of these thatched huts were square and some were circular. The most important place outside the church, which was often built of stone, was the scriptorium, where manuscripts were copied, for the Irish were great lovers of learning. There were farmer monks, gardener monks, monks who were smiths and monks who were carpenters. There was a long room where the monks ate and one monk would have taken the role of cook. There was also a guest house, which was at the door of the monastery. These monks were wise men and very learned and they would have been on good terms with the local kings. In fact, they gave the chieftains advice and must have been well versed in civil law.

Visitors and pilgrims were always well received. Their feet were washed in warm water and they were fed well. They would carry all the news to the monastery and no doubt were called upon to relate their adventures to a rapt audience. Poets were particularly well received, and for a good reason. If a poet was not looked after, they could do a person's reputation grievous harm if they did not meet their approval.

Order was the first law of a monastery and each monk had some practical work to do. There was land to be tilled, fish to be caught, vegetables to be cultivated. Then there were the ordered prayers of the day: at the sound of a bell the monks prayed the psalms. In John Ryan's book *Irish Monasticism*, he speaks about the daily work undertaken by monks:

> Amongst the Irish monks manual labour likewise had an important place; for the principle is clearly stated that, 'The monk is fed and clothed by the labour of his hands.' The different tasks were assigned by a special officer, who was changed from time to time. Work began in the early morning when the brethren betook themselves, each to his allotted duty. First of all came the claims of agriculture in its various branches, ploughing, sowing, reaping, winnowing, and transporting hay and oats back to the barn. The cows, too, had to be milked, the mill and the kiln attended to. The cook, and the baker, and, no doubt, the carpenter and the smith were constantly occupied, whilst chariots or boats might require to be got ready for a journey. Then there were ditches to be dug and roads to be repaired … Fishing, brewing, and bee-keeping might keep one or more of the brethren busy.
>
> (Ryan, J., *Irish Monasticism Origins and Early Development*. Talbot Press Limited: Dublin, 1931.)

There is no doubt that the monastery of those days was busier than the county council offices and the county council yard.

Mayo Abbey

Its present condition belies the fact that Mayo Abbey was hugely important in its day. The monastic enclosure once covered twenty-eight acres and with endowments it eventually owned 2,000 acres. This area became known as

Mayo Abbey.

Mayo of the Saxons. The English monks of Boffin settled here after a dispute with the Irish monks of Inishbofin. This was St Colman's decision. In time it became one of the most important ecclesiastical foundations in the country and some of the Saxon kings were educated here. Venerable Bede praised the monastery, and Alcuin, an English scholar who revised the liturgy of the Frankish Church, wrote a letter to Bishop Leuthfriht about the monastery. Later it became a college and, in around 1370, it adopted the Augustinian rule, surviving until the dissolution of monasteries. It is believed that if it were carefully excavated, a monastery as extensive and important as Clonmacnoise would be revealed. There are several well-carved stones strewn about the cemetery area and the field beside it seems to cover extensive ruins. Until the area is excavated, we cannot be entirely sure of the story of Mayo Abbey.

Claremorris

Claremorris, or in Irish Clár Clainne Mhuiris (the plain of the family of Maurice), takes its name from the famous Norman invader Maurice de Prendergast. He arrived in Ireland with the Norman warlord Strongbow in 1170 and was later granted a large portion of lands in these parts. Local tradition has it that his son Gerald or one of his descendents built the thirteenth-century Brize castle, near Balla. Historically the town is young, but the area has sufficient archaeological remains to indicate that the area has been inhabited for thousands of years. Claremorris was not originally on any principal road or trade route, it is likely that a charter of old fairs was granted in the early seventeenth century.

During the early nineteenth century, Claremorris was tightly controlled by the notorious and feared High Sheriff of Mayo, Denis Browne MP (1763–1828) – no relation to the Castlemagarrett Brownes – who was the resident magistrate and local landlord living at Claremount House. He acquired the rather gruesome nickname of 'Donnchadha an Ropa' (Denis of the rope), as a result of his ruthless treatment of 1798 rebels.

The Right Honourable Denis Browne was High Sheriff of Co. Mayo in 1798. He was a brother of Lord Altamont and dealt savagely with those who had participated in the rising or had helped in any way. It was said that for months afterwards, he had a man hanged in Castlebar each day. Sometimes he presided personally at the executions.

Richard Jordan of Rooskey led the capture of Claremorris with Séamas Bán Ó Máille. Jordan was informed on but Denis Browne, in a letter to Lord Hardwick, said that it would be difficult to find an unprejudiced jury to try him. A court martial was arranged and Jordan was sentenced to death. Browne arranged the execution for Claremorris, where the prisoner had committed the acts of treason. He then added, in his letter to the Lord

Pleasant square, Claremorris.

Lieutenant, 'I shall not fail to attend there and will further your Excellency's intention of making the example as impressive as possible.' The Secret Service List shows that the informer who betrayed Richard Jordan was paid 100 guineas. It was estimated that Denis Browne had 200 men hanged, 200 transported and 100 more pressed into service in the British army overseas or in salt mines on the continent.

In its time Claremorris has produced some interesting people. Claremorris native Cardinal John Francis D'Alton was Archbishop of Armagh and Primate of Ireland between 1946 and 1963. He was born in Claremorris on 11 October 1882. He attended Blackrock College, Dublin and later studied in Clonliffe College. He was ordained in Rome on 18 April 1908 where he did his doctorate of divinity. He continued his studies at Oxford and Cambridge and was an accomplished classical scholar. He became professor of ancient classics at Maynooth and in 1936 became president of the university. Bishop D'Alton was appointed Archbishop of Armagh and Primate of Ireland on 25 April 1946, and on 12 January 1953 he was elevated to the College of Cardinals by Pope Pius XII. His published works include *Horace and His Age*, and *Roman Literary Theory and Criticism: A Study in Tendencies*.

Sir John Grey (1816-1875), also a native of Claremorris, was born at Mount Street in 1816. He studied medicine in Glasgow University and graduated in 1863. On his return to Dublin he turned his attention to journalism, however, and became political editor for the *Freeman's Journal* and later its sole proprietor. He was the trusted advisor and close friend of O'Connell in the struggle for the repeal of the Union.

As a member of Dublin City Council, he advocated the Vartry Water supply for Dublin in 1863. The scheme was implemented in 1863 and he was knighted for his good work. Sir John Gray became Member of Parliament for Kilkenny from 1865 until 1875. His work as MP involved advocating for the disestablishment of the Church of Ireland, reform of land, and education for all denominations. He was elected Lord Mayor of Dublin in 1863 but declined office. He died in Bath, England on 9 April 1875. There is a famous statue close to Trinity College celebrating Sir John Gray for his efforts in bringing a water supply to Dublin in 1868.

Ballindine

We now take the road to Ballindine. Beyond the village is a modern, colourful and playful sculpture called 'The Player' by Ballintubber-based sculptor Cathal McCarthy. It commemorates the life and work of Mr Martin O'Donoghue, the founder of the Disabled Drivers' Association. He was a musician and teacher of music. The sculpture comprises a brightly-coloured steel structure, based on the form of an accordion. It is a joyful thing to observe and has a sense of music and energy.

The sculpture of St Coleman at Claremorris.

Why there is no statue of Patrick Browne in Mayo is something of a mystery. He was not a patriot, a sportsman or a champion. He was a naturalist and he was a friend of Linnaeus.

Patrick Browne, a native of Co. Mayo was born in 1720. He studied medicine in Paris, graduated from the University of Rheims in 1742, and briefly continued his studies at Leiden before practising as a doctor at St Thomas's Hospital, London. Subsequently, he lived for many years in the Caribbean; in Antigua, Jamaica, St Croix and Montserrat, but retired to Co. Mayo in 1771. While he lived in Jamaica, Browne collected fossils, insects, fish and other animals, as well as plants. Ten of his letters to Linnaeus have been preserved. Linnaeus was greatly impressed by Browne's work. He said, 'No author did I ever find quite more instructed.' Asking a friend to pass on a letter to Browne, Linnaeus said, 'Pray be so kind to seal it and send it to the author who has served so much of botanic science beyond all others.' As for Browne himself, Linnaeus said, 'You ought to be honoured with a golden statue.' Browne published *The Civil and Natural History of Jamaica* in 1756, a most significant work in terms of botanical nomenclature, which included new names for 104 genera, and he also planned a volume of medical essays, but this was never printed. Fragments of his essays on venereal disease and yaws have been found among his correspondence with Carl Linnaeus.

His life did not have, as one might expect, long and quiet years during which he could assemble his collections and set them out in a great tome. He married, and his wife was unfaithful to him. Here is a letter he wrote to Linnaeus:

> The pleasure I enjoyed in a Correspondence with you has been for a series of years pass interrupted … In a word I married and the cares of life grew so strong upon me that I could not spare time for any researches in natural history, in hope every year of completing (OK) a modicum that would maintain me genteelly and independent, then to reassume my favourite task. But alas ye best projected sceames sometimes abort and a villain has disconcerted mine. I liv'd many years happily at St Croix in as much business as I could go through and seldom did by less than 3, or, 4 thousand ps per annum until one Juhl a Villain under ye title of Judge had under ye cloak of friendship gott acquainted with my wife and debauched her, as well as some other different families. This obliged me to leave that country and her together; the Danes there are ye most vile wreaches I have ever known and generally combine to keep every foreigner from justice. I am now in Mounteserat a neighbouring island in ye English government.
>
> (Browne, Dr P., *Flowers of Mayo. Dr. Patrick Browne's Fasciculus Plantarum Hiberniae 1788*. Edmund Burke Publisher: Dublin, 1995.)

He returned to Mayo and died at his home in Rushbrook townland on Sunday 29 August 1790. He was buried in the family burial place in Crossboyne, beside his brothers. There is no evidence now of the family burial place within the graveyard at Crossboyne.

Éamonn de Búrca produced *Flowers of Mayo* from the manuscripts that were left behind. It is a sumptuous and limited edition of some 150 copies and is a testament to the great botanist. No statue, despite Linnaeus' wishes, had been erected to him in Mayo.

Close by is the neat village of Irishtown. It became famous during the years of the Land League. What follows is part of an article I wrote about the day that a meeting was held at this village.

Irishtown 1879

The meeting at Irishtown was to change everything. A great landlord was not attacked. In fact he was a small landlord and he was a canon of the Catholic Church. His name was Canon Geoffrey Burke and he was parish priest of Irishtown, which is in west Mayo. His brother had died and he had become the owner of a small estate. His brother had imposed heavy rent on the people and the canon continued to do so.

James Daly, the proprietor of the *Connaught Telegraph*, had begun the year with some fiery words on the state of the country, 'Will the year be as fertile as its predecessor in disappointments? Will the police be sent by their inspectors on Sunday to our chapels not to pray but to take notes of what the priests may say to the oppressed peasantry?' And again, 'Why should honest sons of the soil forever remain ill fed, ill clad, hard-working slaves turning their sweat and toil into money to pay enormous rents without making a rational effort to shake them off?'

James Daly had already urged farmers to hold a mass meeting at Irishtown to protest against a landowner called Canon Burke. On coming into his property Canon Burke had found his tenants in arrears. He promptly threatened people with eviction. No one would touch the case because the landlord was a priest. There was the fear that to attack a priest might bring down a clerical storm but Daly and Davitt were never afraid of such things. They were later to fall into dispute over who organised the meeting and the part played by each one. James Daly was chairman for the occasion.

It was a well-organised event and a glorious day to look back upon later. In a sense it was the beginning of the end for landlordism in Ireland but it did not appear as such at the time.

Demonstrators came from all quarters with their banners and their sashes and their placards. They came by horse and by horse car and many walked. It was one of the greatest demonstrations witnessed in the west of Ireland.

The report in the *Connaught Telegraph* runs as follows:

One of the greatest public demonstrations ever witnessed in the West of Ireland took place on Sunday last at Irishtown near Claremorris. At about one o'clock a monster contingent on horseback drew up in front of Hugh's Hotel, showing discipline and order that a cavalry regiment might be proud of. They were led in sections, each having a marshal who kept his troop well in hand ... James Daly presided. He said, 'We have had a succession of bad crops during the past ten years and the prospect of the eleventh are anything but prominent. You have had a reduction of 35 to 50 per cent on the value of your products within the last five years and yet no reduction of rents have been made.'

There were other speakers on the platform on that day and many resolutions were passed. The other speakers were O'Connor Power, John Ferguson, Thomas Brennan, James Jouden, Matthew Harris and Malachy O'Sullivan. Many would have been Fenians and sympathetic with the Fenian movement. Many slogans are still recalled from that meeting. They would be used again and again. They gave the small tenant a voice, a cause and cohesion. He was no longer alone and fearful of the bailiff and the crowbar brigade.

'You may get a federal parliament, perhaps repeal the union, nay more you may establish and Irish republic on Irish soil but as long as the tillers of the soil are forced to support a useless and indolent aristocracy your federal parliament would be a bauble and your Irish republic but a fraud.'

Those who spoke from the platform that day were protected by five hundred mounted men, so it was a sight to behold.

These words had been uttered before, but on this occasion something happened. The meeting had an immediate effect. Prior to the mass meeting in Irishtown Canon Burke had already lowered the rents by 25 per cent. The news spread like wildfire in Mayo. A chink had appeared in the landlord system. Rents began to fall all over the county. It all began at Irishtown.

Ballyhaunis

Ballyhaunis is the most eastern of our towns. The light of morning, therefore, first shines on Ballyhaunis. There is a mosque in this town, the most westerly mosque in Europe. There is a well-integrated Muslim community here and Halal meats are processed in the town. Here also are the headquarters of Midwest radio. In the old days, when local radio broadcasts were of dubious provenance, a radio station was set up here. It is both homely and universal and presided over by Paul Claffey. At the end of the town there is an Augustinian priory, which incorporates fragments of an Augustinian friary dedicated to the Blessed Virgin Mary. The friary was founded in 1430. The only remains of the ancient buildings consist of the walls of a church connected to two wings by arches. The archaeological evidence points to intense inhabitation here during prehistoric times.

One of the Friars at Ballyhaunis was Fair Cassidy or, in Irish, An Caisideach Bán. He is a very interesting man who possessed a tormented soul. Ó Caisaide was probably born in Roscommon and ordained an Augustinian friar. It is likely that he was defrocked on account of a love affair with a young girl who may have been the one addressed in 'Máire Bhéil Átha hAmhnais', the folksong attributed to him. A group of love songs were created based on this talk of love between a young girl and her confessor, including those to which Douglas Hyde gave the collective title *An Caisideach, Bán nó An Bráthair Buartha* – 'The Fair Cassidy, or The Troubled Friar' – in *The Religious Songs of Connaught*. The well-known song 'Carrickfergus' recalls these circumstances in some of its verses. According to one story he left for France, joined the French army, but deserted it. He then spent some time in Hamburg, before returning to Ireland living as a wandering storyteller. This great poem gives us an idea of his tempestuous life:

Midwest Radio Headquarters.

An Caisideach Bán (The Fair Cassidy)

> I wandered down from the top of the Reek,
> Down to you, over at Sliabh Bán,
> In search of the girl who left my mind troubled,
> And who turned my heart as black as coal;
> My shoulders swelled up to my ears
> And I received a clear sharp warning from death;
> And there wasn't one who heard my story,
> Who didn't say that he'd pity the Caisideach Bán.
> (Kenny, A., An Caisideach Bán *The songs and adventures of Tomás Ó Caiside.*
> Greensprint Ltd.: Ballyhaunis, 1993.)

This is only part of the magnificent poem, which belongs to medieval European civilisation. His adventures in Europe are of heroic proportions and as Adrian Kenny remarks in his fine book *The songs and adventures of Tomás Ó Caiside*, they could run in to one thousand pages of memoir. Here is an extract about part of his journey through Europe:

> Afterwards we came in custody of the enemy, in the Black Forest, as they call it, where we were kept prisoner for three long autumn days. We got good quarters from Prince Alexander and after that from Prince Eugene. We sold our horses and our arms except for our swords and pocket pistols. We got a pass through the territory from the great princes I've mentioned, and a pocketful of silver. Gratefully we travelled through this rough, tangled, impassable country,

Ancient medieval doorway in
Ballyhaunis.

through lonely, deserted glens, through thick, horrible, bright-wattled woods
full of wild beasts; listening to the screaming of wild boar, the howling of wild
dogs, the shrill whistle of serpents and the deep musical sounds of spectres
and monsters; and the shepherds sound their bugles and horns, seeking where
they would lead their flocks in the morning for quarter and in the evening for
shelter in the woods; until we travelled every strange place from Sanhausen to
Langernam near Friezleir on the edge of Marburg in the rough furzy land of
Hanover, where I left my friend and travelling companion.
(Kenny, A., An Caisideach Bán *The songs and adventures of Tomás Ó Caiside.*
Greensprint Ltd.: Ballyhaunis,1994.)

We know very little of his wandering life in Ireland and when or where he
died. His emotional energy was immense, his lusts troubling to him, and he
could not rest in any single place. Adrian Kenny did us a great literary service
in restoring his work to the public.

William John Francis Naughton, or Bill Naughton (1910-1992) was a British playwright and author, best known for his play *Alfie*. He also helped to create *Coronation Street*. Born in Ballyhaunis in 1910, his family moved to Bolton in Lancashire in 1914, where he attended St Peter and Paul School. Naughton worked as a weaver, coal-bagger and lorry-driver before he started to write.

He wrote about Bolton and other subject matter that he knew. His style was easy and transparent. Naughton's preferred environment was working-class society. Although *Alfie* is the play with which he will always be associated, mostly because of the British film starring Michael Caine, he was a prolific writer, with many plays, novels, short stories and children's books to his name. At least two of his other plays have been transferred onto the cinema screen. These are *Spring and Port Wine*, which starred James Mason in the role of Rafe Crompton, and *The Family Way*, which starred John Mills. His work also includes the novel *One Small Boy*, and the collection of short stories *The "Goalkeeper's Revenge" and Other Stories*.

Bill Naughton died in 1992, in Ballasalla on the Isle of Man. There is today a 'Bill Naughton Short Story Competition' in honour of the author. Each year at Aghamore, close to Ballyhaunis, the life of Bill Naughton is celebrated. It is a unique occasion and some of the best writers in the British Isles have slipped into the village, read their works and enjoyed each other's company. It is held in a small, whitewashed house with a turf fire blazing in the grate. Every year, an ancient pub is reactivated. It has not been renovated, has no pretensions, and makes no concessions to modern times.

It also celebrates P.D. Kenny (1862-1944) who was a journalist, author and farmer who wrote under the pseudonym 'Pat'. He was born in Lismagansion, Aghamore. He was an interesting and enigmatic figure although his involvement in several political and ecclesiastical controversies, together with various court cases, made him unpopular with some segments of Irish society.

Charlestown and Knock

In the 1840s the land occupied by what is now Charlestown was a bog. Stepping stones across what is now known as the Roundabout, led to the ancient town of Bellaghy, just across the county border in Co. Sligo. The Mayo tenants of the Lord Dillon Estate had to carry their sacks of potatoes and grain there on market days. Because they were Mayo men and tenants of Lord Dillon, they were forced to wait at the weighing scales until all the Sligo men had their produce weighed.

The Mayo tenants complained bitterly to the agent of Lord Dillon, Charles Strickland, who protested to the Lord of Sligo estate. He was rebuffed, but it was not until later, when Strickland was publicly insulted, that he swore vengeance. He vowed to wipe out Bellaghy. With the consent of Lord Dillon, Strickland immediately offered a large holding of rent-free land forever to the man or woman who would build the first house in what would be a new town. Many accepted the invitation.

One July day in 1846, the labourers and builders employed by the Henry family looked across at their opponents and began to worry. Their opponents now had rafters in place and were calling for the slates in order to be able to finish the work. Henry's men decided to make a daring move: they would have to delay that cargo of slates to the Mulligan family. Michael Henry (who hailed from Swinford and married Mary Mulligan, whose father John Mulligan gave the young couple the gift of the site) had his men go to Swinford, and meet the carters who were bringing the slates from the port of Ballina. There, they entertained the carters, plied them with all the drink they needed and made them forget about delivering the slates at the required time. While the workers on the Mulligan house sat about waiting for the slates, the men on Henry's house worked around the clock to slate their roof and light a fire. They completed the first house, won the race and claimed the land that went with it.

The area developed quickly and established itself as a town and Bellaghy is still on the map today. In Bellaghy, counties Mayo and Sligo run into each other, and you will not know when you step from one into the other. At the centre of the town stands an artistic triangle, where three granite sheep graze forever.

If the journalist John Healy were alive today he would be surprised at many things. Firstly, that Knock Airport succeeded beyond expectation. Secondly, by the building boom in Mayo, and he would be surprised at how easily and confidently we now move about the world.

John Healy was an interesting man. He was born in Charlestown and started work with the *Western People*. He went to Dublin and became an influential journalist. His column 'Backbencher' was to change Irish journalism, in that it opened the doors of parliament and the cabinet table to the general reader. His style was direct and hard-hitting and as a result his column was eagerly read every Saturday. His small book *No One Shouted Stop!* was extremely influential; in it he cried out against mass emigration, the destruction of the small farmer, the depopulation of the province, the destruction of the old rural rituals and the improper growth of Dublin. He describes the dark days, when little stirred in the town except on Dole days:

> 'You remember Jimmy Foley, the baker, who was always good for 'the odd clod' to make up fourpence.'
> 'How is Jimmy Foley now?' you ask.
> 'He's beyond in England these fourteen years. 'My brother is a little amazed I did not know.'
> 'And Mrs Foley – is she in Barrach Street still?'
> 'No; they all cleared out to England.'
> You name a dozen other in Barrack Street who were men when you were a boy and they are gone; you name those who were boys in school with you and they are gone, married and settled in England, America, or Australia or Canada, wherever the English language was spoken. And you come back to Paddy Casey's which has shut down so peremptorily and you are forced to say.
> 'The town is really getting shook, isn't it?'
> (Healy, J., *No One Shouted Stop*. House of Healy: Achill, 1988.)

But no one knows how the wheels of fortune change, and change they did for Charlestown. With the establishment of Knock Airport and the advance of education, all things changed. Now Knock International Airport stands upon a hill at Barna Cuige. It was built on faith, helped along by an energetic priest, Monsignor Horan. Now in Charlestown the shop fronts are brightly painted, there are large supermarkets, delis with exotic food, and there is a bustling energy in the town.

If you are entering Mayo for a brief holiday or returning from England to see your family you will come by Knock International Airport. Knock gets its name from the Irish 'cnoc' which means hill. This airport is one of the friendliest in Ireland. It was an extraordinary place to build an airport. The top of a hill was removed in the same way as ones removes the top of an egg, and a runway set out. Since its opening, the airport has expanded enormously. At night the lights of Knock Airport shine over what was once known as the Black Triangle.

Knock Airport owes its conception to Knock Shrine. Today the shrine is a great cathedral, with a thin spire breaking the flat skyline. The houses in the area are new and prosperous, and the souvenir shops are modern and thriving. The place bustles with people and the roads in and out of Knock are wide, straight and well maintained. There are always pilgrims at Knock, wheeling about the chapel, kneeling in front of the wall where the apparitions took place.

It was not the most pleasant place when Archdeacon Kavanagh became parish priest there. It was raining on the evening of 21 August 1879 and, according to witnesses, at 8p.m. the Virgin Mary, together with St Joseph and St John the Evangelist, appeared to local people. The apparitions were against the rough, uncemented gable of the church. According to fifteen local

Knock Airport: Monsignor Horan's dream fulfilled.

witnesses, despite the rain, the visibility of the apparitions was not impaired.

From the official account, the first person to notice anything unusual was Margaret Byrne. She saw a strange brightness over the church. Mary McLoughlin, coming home from her holidays in Lecanvey, also perceived this brightness. She saw the figures at the gable end of the church and thought that the archdeacon had purchased some statues. Others began to gather and noted that the figures were moving and the earth beneath them was dry. They were full and round as if they had bodies and life. A man half a mile away saw the light at the back of the church. Rain was falling heavily at the time on the people, but no rain fell where the figures were. The housekeeper later told the archbishop, but he paid little attention to what had happened. He thought it was probably a trick of the light.

All those who saw the vision were questioned about what they saw and their testimony is readily available. Mary O'Connell was examined under oath when she was eighty-six. She was questioned in her bedroom as she was too ill to leave. She ended her description of what she saw on 21 August with these solemn words, 'I am clear about everything I have said and I make this statement knowing I am going before my God.' She died later that year, on 19 October 1937.(Rynne, C., *Knock 1879-1979*. Veritas Publications, 1979)

The news spread across the countryside, as such news always does. People began to come in crowds. In October, Dr McHale set up an official inquiry. A formidable group of priests gathered for the purpose. They were well versed in theology and philosophy and were all men of the world. Two accounts of the day-long commission were published. The testimony of Bridget Trench, aged seventy-five was delivered in Irish. Mary O'Connell was the last surviving witness of the apparition. Fifteen witnesses were examined and the Commission reported that the 'testimony' of all taken, as a whole, was trustworthy and satisfactory. Then, in 1936, Archbishop Gilmartin set up another commission to examine the three surviving witnesses of the apparition: Mrs Mary O'Connell (*née* Byrne), Patrick Byrne and John Curry. All three confirmed their original statements of 1879.

The verdict of this commission was that the evidence of the witnesses was upright and trustworthy, and concerning Mrs O'Connell it was reported that she left a most favourable impression on their minds. On 30 September 1979 Pope John Paul II came to Knock as a pilgrim.

Monsignor Horan is buried in the grounds, close to the cathedral. Had he been a businessman he would have been a multimillionaire. He might not have blessed the top of a high hill with holy water and pronounced that from

The Cathedral in Knock.

Apparition gable end at Knock.

this bog would rise an airport, but he helped miracles along with his business and political acumen. His vision was broad; he built an airport, he built a cathedral, he cleaned up the traders' shops at Knock, and he invited a pope to Ireland. He was greatly admired and we all had a great regard for him. He was, as they say, a bit of a rogue; he could twist arms, generate political consensus and smile in a knowing way when he was interviewed by television crews, but he was a pious man who enjoyed the life of a religious entrepreneur.

We now return to Charlestown and take the road to Swinford. Some years ago Brabazon House still stood firmly, close to the golf club. The town of Swinford owes its origins to the Brabazons, who had been given land in the parish of Kilconduff during the Cromwellian settlement. They originally came to Ballinasloe from Leicester in England. They became landlords for Swinford and the surrounding district. Colonel John Brabazon was the last of his family and he sold his estate to the Congested Board. He died in Switzerland in 1923. He was a friend of the Churchill family and it was a friendship that Churchill cherished. It was obvious that the great days of the landlords were over and a long twilight was to follow.

The Brabazons were dispossessed of their castle and lands at Ballinasloe on 12 August 1652 and Anthony Brabazon then fled to Spain. His son George and his wife Sarah Burke from Galway came to Kilconduff and built the Brabazon house and stables in Swinford. Their son Anthony inherited the estate and married Anne Moyneux in 1776. The Cromwellian plantation affected almost 1,000 royalist families. It was payback for his soldiers and his captains. They were given the best of the land and there was a vast migration westwards. Many Anglo-Irish families ended up on bad land. In this way, it seems, the Brabazon family was carried west on this historic wave. Here is a description of this distinguished gentleman, Sir John Palmer, Major-General Brabazon, the last of the line:

> Two soldiers figured importantly in Winston's military career. They were named, euphoniously, Bindon Blood and John Brabazon. Colonel Brabazon, as he was when Winston first met him, was a penurious Irish landlord, with an inherited passion for horses, and the army. He was a fine-looking man, with a tremendous moustache, piercing grey eyes and grey curly hair parted in the middle. He affected the style of the dandy, processed through the season, through the Court and through club land, with stately grace and was never heard to pronounce an 'r' in his life. 'Where is the London twain?' he once asked the Aldershot stationmaster. And when told it had left: 'Gone! Bwing another.'

Hospital at Swinford.

Brabazon knew everyone, was an intimate of the Prince of Wales, and possessed charm and conversational powers which attracted all the most beautiful of his time, thought he abstained from marriage. His courage and military record, when there was little enough campaigning to be had, were impeccable. His broad chest was ablaze with medals and clasps. He was also well-read, which was about as rare a quality in the army as his own appointment, through the intervention of the Prince of Wales, as Colonel of the 4th Hussars over the heads of long-serving officers of that regiment.

(Hough, R., *Winston and Clementine*. Bantam Press: London, 1990.)

Sir William Brabazon died a bachelor while dining at his own table, having choked on a chicken bone on 24 October 1840 aged sixty-two. He was buried in the family vault under the Church of Ireland church.

Part of the old workhouse in Swinford still exists. It is now a small hospital. But at the gates of this workhouse the hungry crowded during the terrible famine of 1846 to 1849. Behind the hospital is a mound surrounded by a stone wall, where the famine victims were buried. Michael Davitt, whom we will meet when we reach Straide, wrote this of the workhouse:

Swinford Workhouse was our destination after being evicted, and there we presented ourselves the same day, the family consisting of six persons; my father, mother, three sisters, aged respectively eight, three years, two months and I, being the second eldest, four and a half years old, at the time. Fortunately for our brief stay within such a place one of the regulations required that male children above three years of age should be kept apart from their mothers – for what reason or purpose I know not; but when this condition of enjoying workhouse hospitality was mentioned to my mother she snatched me to her breast, and declaring she would rather die by the roadside than submit to such and inhuman condition, left the establishment, inside the walls of which we had stayed but one hour.

(Davitt, M., and King, C., *Jottings in Solitary*. University College Dublin Press, Dublin, 2004.)

Many noble families had to flee abroad or endure life on marginal land. Some became outlaws or rapparees. Many rapparee bands operated in Ireland well into the eighteenth century. Famous figures among them include Count Redmond O'Hanlon, and Eamonn Ryan – also known as Éamonn an Chnoic, or 'Ned of the Hill', who entered Irish folklore through songs and poems about his exploits.

There was one such rapparee operating in the Swinford area called Gallagher. His many deeds are still remembered in the folklore of the area. He committed robberies on the open roads and at night he attacked the estates of the landlords. He hid in various locations in the area and found refuge in woods close to Knock. Gallagher had a residence on Glass Island near Pontoon. He escaped arrest many times before his eventual capture. According to local legend, he was staying in a local house while recovering from an illness. He was given a meal, which had been laced with poitín, after which he fell asleep. The family then got to work and put him to bed beside the fire. His ankles and wrists were tied with flax ropes and a message was sent to the Redcoats in Foxford, who in turn alerted Ballina, Swinford and Castlebar. Captain Gallagher, already bound, was taken to Castlebar to be hanged after a hasty trial.

We travel now to Hennigan's Heritage Centre at Killasser. Hennigan's Heritage Centre is situated in unspoilt countryside overlooking Creagaballa Lake, four miles from the workhouse at Swinford where thousands of people from the region died from starvation during the nineteenth century, and twelve miles from The Museum of Country Life, Turlough. I spent a most pleasant day here with the journalist Tom Shiels.

It is truly a wonderful place. Tom, without government aid and without the blast of trumpets, has built up one of the finest folk museums in the

Swinford Railway Station.

county. He is a learned man, friendly, energetic and with darting eyes. He has built up this museum over many years and set it out to his own design. He is curator, collector and guide, and has done a great service to his county.

We have travelled far and we might as well rest in Swinford. It is decently quiet in the evening time and the great and burdensome trucks no longer shake the old foundations of the town. At the end of the town a fine railway bridge arches over the road and leads to Foxford.

Attymass lies in rugged country, sheltering at the foot of the Ox Mountains. It is the birthplace of Fr Patrick Peyton, the world-famous founder of the Family Rosary Crusade. It has been marked by its history with crannogs, ring forts, megalithic tombs, court tombs and ancient cooking sites. It is a landscape of small limestone fields and small woods, tough grass and heather, and looks down upon Mayo. In the distance lies the majestic profile of Nephin Mountain. It has a great tradition of scholarship and amongst its many luminaries was Fr Payton. He was born here in 1902 and he died in 1992. He was ordained a Holy Cross priest in 1941. A highly intelligent, zealous, and charismatic man, it was his firm belief that the Virgin Mary had saved him in his youth from a nearly fatal illness. He devoted his life to the mission of enhancing family life by regular use of the rosary. His gospel, reflecting his own humility and simplicity, was, 'The family that prays together stays together.'

The hindquarters of the Ox Mountains.

From a high hill you will see the Meelick Round Tower. It stands in a cemetery, on a ridge, to the right of the road in the village itself. It still possesses four windows with lintells. The tower lacks its cap and traditional bell-storey and it is level at the top. With its abundant lichen growth, the tower seems to glow in sunlight as well as under floodlights at night. To the right and at the foot of the tower is an old Irish cross-slab bearing interlacing ornaments and the old Irish inscription *OR DO GRICOUR* meaning 'a prayer for Gricour'. It is believed that there had been an ancient monastic site on these grounds. This countryside yields up its secrets slowly, for one has to search in many places for its history.

Foxford and Straide

At Foxford the River Moy runs beneath an ancient bridge and then it is shredded on razor-sharp rocks as it rushes past the famous woollen mills. Formerly, Foxford blankets were famous all over the world. They were part of the substance of the land and it was felt that if Foxford could be imitated, then each small town in Ireland could be rejuvenated and people could remain at home and work from there. Today the mills are closed and the great machines are silent. The mills have been replaced by an attractive shop, a small museum and a quaint tea house. There are plans for great developments here, based around the memory of Admiral Brown, the founder of the Argentinean navy and defender of a new country.

Like all other landscapes in Mayo, Foxford was marked by early Stone Age people. They made their way along the Moy River system, where they found fuel, prey and berries in the woods, along with rivers and lakes which were full of fish. Evidence of such habitations turns up continually in this area.

But definite information on the area begins with the Norman Jordan family. The origin of the name is romantic, stemming from one Jordan De Exeter, who acquired estates in Ireland following the Norman Invasion of 1172. It is said that a Norman knight brought back bottles of water from the River Jordan and used it to baptise his children, whom he thereafter named Jordan. The name in Irish, McSíurtáin, denotes one who was a 'descendent of Jordan'. The ruins of the Ballylahan castle, the seat of the Mayo Jordans, still stands alongside the junction of the N58 from Ballyvary to Ballina and the R321 which links Straide with Bohola. Ballylahan Castle is an imposing building to this day. It dominates the area and is an ever-present reminder of the presence of the Jordan family. It is still a formidable building and on a misty day in autumn, with the trees bare, is possesses an Arthurian charm.

Top: Winter landscape in Foxford.

Above: The church at Foxford.

Right: Admiral Brown, founder of the Argentinean navy.

To protect the flank of their properties it is said that a castle was built at Foxford where the mills now stand. Towns often developed at fords, for this is where people chose to pass with their cattle and horses on their way to fairs. It was also a place where an army might find safe crossing into the Jordan territory. Foxford became a military town. When the French invasion took place the army set up a barricade in the town in expectation of a battle. But Humbert swung away from the town and no battle took place.

William Brown, the founder of the Argentinean navy, was born here in 1777. In 1786 his family emigrated to America where Brown worked as a cabin boy. During the war between France and England, his ship, an English merchantman, was captured by a French privateer and he was made prisoner of war. After re-entering the ocean trade, his ship was wrecked on the coast of South America. Here he established the first regular packet service between Buenos Aires and Montevideo. In the revolt of Buenos Aires against Spain the insurgents appointed Brown to the command of a squadron of seven ships. On St Patrick's Day he captured the fort of Martín García, called 'The Gibraltar of the La Plata', compelling nine Spanish men-of-war under Admiral Romerate to retire. Here is an account of the battle from *Admiral Brown* by Marcos Aguinis:

And so, on 10 March 1814, the battle begins. It lasts until the following morning. Brown launches an assault on the island stronghold of Martín García because it represents a strategic gateway to the inland waterways. The batteries spit out an angry rebuff and soon a dense cloud of smoke envelopes the battle zone. The *Hércules* manoeuvres to avoid the hail of shot, but she runs aground on a sandbank and quickly becomes the main target of the enemy. For hours she endures an unrelenting barrage. Her decks run with blood as one-quarter of her men fall … When the *Hércules* struggles to free herself from the sandbank, the rest of the fleet is pounded as it tries to distract Romarte from the beleaguered ships … At dusk the firing ceases. On the deck of the *Hércules* lie dozens of men, dead or wounded. Brown walks among the stricken, distributing water, rum and words of encouragement. He was yet ready to retire. He will fight his way out of this … Even now, Brown does not flinch. He remembers his uncle and his stories of Ireland's patron saint, St Patrick, who managed to convert a pagan nation to Christianity against all the odds. The date today is 15 March, two days before St Patrick's feast day. Inspired, Brown rushes to the piper and drummer and orders them to play 'St Patrick's Day in the morning'. His troops, many of them Irish, rouse themselves with a tremendous effort rush

forward, finally succeeding in over-running the defences of Martín García …
Romarte is running low on ammunition and opts to retreat to Montevideo.
On seeing this, the Argentineans erupt in a deafening roar of triumph. They
wave handkerchiefs, bandages, arms, flags; they hug each other, sing, howl. The
Hércules is refloated and, drunk with joy, they sail to the nationalist port of
Colonia for repairs.
(Aquinis, M., *Admiral William Brown*. The Admiral Brown Society: Foxford, 2006.)

As the hero of the action, Brown was raised to the rank of colonel and made
commander of the navy. His flagship, the *Hercules*, was presented to him as a
personal gift and reward for his services.

He was to return to Mayo in 1847 and to visit Foxford. He gave money
for the relief of the poor and met a brother who did not recognise him. After
a visit to his native land, Admiral Brown returned to Argentina and spent his
last years quietly. He died in Buenos Aires on 3 May 1867, and in the Recolta
cemetery a lofty column marks his resting place. His greatness is gradually
being recognised in Ireland. It is chiefly through J.J. O'Hara, who is known
in Argentina as 'Loco Juan José' (Crazy John Joseph) – that the importance of
Admiral William Brown is being recognised and honoured. The publication
of the book *Liberator of the South Atlantic* by Marcos Aguinis, who is one of
the finest writers in Argentina, will hurry this process forward. His life was
heroic, tragic, tempestuous, filled with adventure and danger, and he is greatly
honoured in Argentina, with 500 statues and over 1,000 streets named after
him. Football teams, as well as towns, are called after him too:

On 3 March 1857 the pearly head of the Admiral lies still forever. The birds
cry out, announcing the death of a sailor who has traversed the waters of the
world, from Foxford to Philadelphia, from the Atlantic to the Rhine, from the
Thames to El Plata, from Cape Horn to the Galapagos from the River Guayas
to the Antilles. The mourners start to arrive; peasants, dignitaries, friends,
clerics, officers. The governor of Buenos Aires signs a decree of honours …
The coffin of Brown is resplendent, draped with his dress uniform and the
sword presented to him by Robert Ramsay, and it is accompanied on its final
voyage by his military decorations and the flag from the Battle of Los Pozos
… There in the chapel, Fr Anthony Fahy delivers the funeral service. Then
Brown is interred alongside the tomb of General José María Paz. From afar,
the cannons of the squadrons bid farewell to the first Admiral of the Republic.
Mitre, delivers a vibrant elegy.

Brown in life, standing on the quarterdeck of his ship was worth as much as a fleet to us.

(Aquinis, M., *Admiral William Brown*. The Admiral Brown Society: Foxford, 2006.)

The famine blighted land through which Admiral Brown passed on his way to Foxford. The famine was particularly terrible in Mayo, and Foxford did not escape its horrors. The wretched weather seemed to join forces with the potato blight to destroy the inhabitants of Mayo. There were reports about the bad weather from all over the county in the local papers. With the famine came the fever, which swept people away. The poor had no protection and were the worst affected. They lived for most of the year on the potato, the most nutritious of foods. The population had exploded and the land had been divided again and again by families. The poorhouses at Ballina and Swinford were completely overcrowded. The hungry waited at the gates for those within to die in order to gain entrance.

The famine passed in Foxford. It left the town depleted and without energy. Agnes Morrogh-Bernard, of Foxford, was a nun of outstanding merit and vision. She was a very practical Christian. She came from an upper-class family and was educated at home and at Laurel Hill Convent in Limerick. She completed her education in Paris and on her return, after her twenty-first birthday, she entered the novitiate and became a nun, taking four vows; the three normal vows of poverty, chastity and obedience and the vow of helping the poor. Shortly afterwards she was given a teaching post in Gardener Street School and some months later was sent to King's Inn School. In April 1877, Agnes, now known as Mother Arsenius Morrogh-Bernard, arrived in Ballaghaderreen.

During her years in Ballaghaderreen it was stressed to Agnes that a convent was needed in Foxford and so in 1890, with the help of a friend and assistance from the local sergeant, a house was found. On 9 December 1890, Mother Morrogh-Bernard and one sister came to live in Foxford. She set up the woollen mills on the east bank of the Moy. In an effort to further her plans for a woollen mills in Foxford, Mother Morrogh-Bernard made contact with the great champion of the west, Michael Davitt, and through his office obtained the name of a certain Mr Charles Smith, of Caledon Mills in Co. Tyrone. Smith's response to Mother Morrogh-Bernard's initial correspondence, although never preserved in the convent archives, became immortalised in the history of Foxford Woollen Mills, 'Madam, are you aware that you have

The River Moy in Foxford.

written to a Protestant and a Freemason?'(Laffey, J., Foxford. *Through the Arches of Time*, Berry Print Group, Westport, 2003.)

Over the next few years a school was built and in 1893 Mother Morrogh-Bernard got a grant so that training could be given in the domestic and farming areas of the community. As the years passed and money became more plentiful she had houses built for employees of the mill. The music school was built in 1923, and later the convent chapel was added. Both of these can still be seen in Foxford today. Up until her death in 1932, Agnes continued to improve and update the mill and the town itself.

The poet, F.R. Higgins was born in Foxford in 1896 but he grew up in Co. Meath. He loved Mayo with a passion and this passion informs his poetry. Yeats, his mentor, introduced him to the Dublin literary circles. He returned to Mayo for a short time with his wife May, who was a harpist. He was associated with the Abbey Theatre and the Cuala Press. Higgins died in 1940 and is buried near Trim in Co. Meath. Frank O'Connor called him 'Falstaffian' as he was jovial and jolly like the Shakespearian character Falstaff. His papers are in the National Library of Ireland.

We pass along the river and set out for Straide. Here, one should visit Straide Abbey and pause at the grave of Mayo's most famous son, Michael Davitt.

The Jordan family, as we have seen, were a powerful Norman family, and the presence of their castles shows how established they were in the area. They were tied to a continental Church and they brought with them continental

Michael Davitt's tomb at Straide.

order. The Franciscans were introduced either by Exeter de Jordan, or by his son. It was, in any case, at the request of Exeter's wife Basilia that they were replaced by the Dominicans. The story goes that Jordan was expecting guests at his castle, and just before they arrived his wife Basilia told him she would refuse to meet them unless the Dominicans were received into Straide – he had to accede to her request. Others say that she refused to eat and drink at the banquet until her wishes were granted.

The Dominicans made their first appearance in Straide in 1252. Soon after, the abbey was burned down and an indulgence for its restoration was granted in 1434. It is said that the *Annals of Multyfarnham*, which are now in Trinity College, were compiled at Straide, as there is frequent reference to the Exeter family in the manuscript.

Michael Davitt was born in Straide. He was born here in 1846 during the Great Famine and he died in Dublin in 1906. His father was a small farmer who was evicted from his home and thrown on to the side of the road.

The family ended up in Haslingden in Lancashire. Michael worked at a cotton mill where he caught his arm in a spinning machine and it had to be amputated. Having recovered from the accident, he began to study at the local school. He was intelligent, like all his family, and developed a great interest in reading. When he had completed his education he went to work in a post

Famous filigree tracery work at Straide Abbey.

office where he learnt to be a typesetter. He began reading extensively and became interested in Irish history. Fenianism was in the air at the time and Davitt decided to become a member of the Irish Republican Brotherhood. He rose through the ranks and became one of the foremost leaders and was involved in smuggling arms into Ireland. As a result of these activities he was captured and thrown in jail. It was in jail that his mind turned to the radical problems of Ireland, and the basic problem of that time was that of land. This would change the course of his life. He describes his life in Dartmoor Prison as follows:

> If the whole United Kingdom was searched through for the purpose of discovering a place whereon to erect a prison, with the view of utilizing the rigours of a severe climate, damp fogs, more than average rainfall, and a lengthening winter season ... no more suitable place than Dartmoor could be found ...
>
> For the first week after my arrival from Millbank I was located in the penal cells. The penal cells are much more preferable to the ordinary or iron cells, being somewhat larger and much better ventilated; but owing to their being

constructed and set apart for incorrigible prisoners – men who are taught obedience by means of starvation, and consequently maddened by hunger and cold – it is almost impossible to obtain any sleep in such a place. The iron or ordinary cell I was next located in, and remained an inmate of for close to five years, I will now describe. Length, seven feet exactly, width, four feet, and height seven feet. The sides of it are of corrugated iron, and the floor is a slate one. These cells are ranged in tiers or wards in the centre of a hall, the tiers being one above the other to the height of four wards ... The sole provision made for ventilating these cells is an opening of two and a half or three inches left at the bottom of each door ... In the heat of summer it was almost impossible to breathe in these top cells; so close and foul would the air become from improper ventilation of the cells below, allowing the breathed air in each cell to mix with that in the hall, and thus ascend to the top ... I was, however, soon removed to a lower tier after foul eruptions began to break out upon my body through the impure air I had been breathing ... I have often, in the summer season, repeatedly to go on my knees and put my mouth to the bottom of the door for a little air.

The light admitted to those ordinary iron cages is scarcely sufficient to read by in the daytime. I have often laid the length of my body on the cell floor, and placed my book under the door to catch sufficient light to read by it.
(Cashman, D.B., *The Life Of Michael Davitt*. Washbourne Ltd. 1881.)

It is said that he learned French while at Dartmoor, from a French prisoner. He was released on a ticket of leave after approximately seven years of hardship. He would later write a book entitled *Leaves from a Prison Diary*. He founded the Land League in Castlebar with James Daly and this was to change the fundamental structure of land possession in Ireland. He was an accomplished and civilised man. He married an American beauty with musical talent and education, named Mary Yore. He made several trips to America to meet his family, where he was received like a celebrity. He also made quick stop tours across America and at all these stops he was fêted and honoured by the Irish Americans. He met everyone of importance in America, and they were most anxious to meet him. He supported many causes and was particularly concerned with the treatment dealt out to prisoners. Oscar Wilde sent him a dedicated copy of *The Ballad of Reading Gaol*, for Oscar had also been acquainted with the inside of prisons. He was interested in education and the necessity of public libraries. He went to South Africa and wrote in favour of the Boers. He travelled to Palestine, went to Cana, Galilee, and Jerusalem and looked upon the Dead Sea. He travelled to Australia and lectured there and on a trip to New Zealand he met Mark Twain with whom he got on famously.

Coming to the end of his days, he visited Tolstoy at his home at Yasnaya Polyana. They got along well together and discussed the problems of the day. It was obvious that Tolstoy was greatly impressed by Davitt. He visited Kishinev in 1903. You will not find Kishinev on the map because today it is called Chisinau; it is the capital of Moldova. The name Kishinev, however, was thrust into the consciousness of the world on Easter Day, 1903, when forty-nine Jews were massacred there by frenzied mobs. Hundreds more were seriously injured; thousands were left homeless and property damage was measured in millions of gold roubles. Public outrage was expressed in protests, which echoed through every civilized capital of the world. Michael Davitt was sent to investigate for the *New York American Journal* soon after the pogrom of 1903. He was a man who could be trusted and he was a writer of international importance. He called the book he published later, *Within the Pale: The True Story of Anti-Semitic Persecutions in Russia* and in it he wrote graphically of what he had witnessed there.

Michael Davitt died at Elpis Nursing Home, Lower Mount Street, Dublin and his final wish to be buried in Straide was set out in his will, which every child in Mayo should know off by heart:

Should I die in Ireland, I would wish to be buried at Straide, Co. Mayo, without any funeral demonstrations. If I die in America, I must be buried in my mother's grave at Manayunk, near Philadelphia, and on no account be brought back to Ireland. If in any other country (outside of Great Britain) to be buried in the nearest graveyard to where I may die, with the simplest possible ceremony. Should I die in Great Britain, I must be buried at Straide, Co. Mayo. My diaries are not to be published as such, and in no instance without my wife's permission; but on no account must anything harsh or censorious written in said diaries by me about any person, dead or alive, who has ever worked for Ireland, be printed, published, or used so as to give pain to any friend or relative. To all my friends I leave kind thought; to my enemies the fullest possible forgiveness; and to Ireland the undying prayers for the absolute freedom and independence which it was my life's ambition to try and obtain for her. I appoint my wife, Mary Davitt, the sole executrix of this will.

Dated the first of February, one thousand nine hundred and four.

Michael Davitt

(Sheehy-Skeffington, F., *Michael Davitt: Revolutionary Agitator and Labour Leader*. Macgibbon & Kee: London, 1908.)

His story of his noble life is written into this final testament. There is much more that could be said of this noble man, but it is time to visit Bellavary.

Once, a small road ran through this little town. Then a great road was opened close by, so in a sense it became an island of tranquillity. One side of my family drank in Bellavary and the other side in Belcarra, so I have a great interest in both places. To me, they are mythological places and have stimulated my imagination as no other places have. I grew up believing that they were populated by magical and mystical characters. Kevin Sykes makes violins close to town, and at Carrowkeel they make furniture, and at Parke, windmills. There are the remnants of a great mill at Bellavary. It has a haunting presence reminiscent of a time when the great wheel, moved by a stream, set the great whetstone in motion to grind corn.

You turn left towards Bohola. Despite its small size Bohola has always been a place of significance. Bohola was the birthplace of the great athlete Martin Sheridan (1881-1918) and there is a memorial in his honour on the village green. Martin won nine Olympic medals (five gold, three silver and one bronze) for his adopted country, the USA, in discus-throwing, high and long jumps, shot put and pole-vaulting at St Louis (1904), Athens (1906) and London (1908).

The area is quite rich in ancestral memory and is associated with many famous people. Bohola people are spread across the world and have an intense connection with their locality.

We pass down the road to Cill Liadáin (or Killedan). It is a place surrounded by deciduous trees and it has an enchanted feeling. Once there was an active monastery there and the ruins suggest that they were important. Leonard Strong purchased land in Killedan and gave it to Emily McManus' grandparents in 1845. Here is how Emily MacManus writes of the area:

> It contained 1,200 acres in all; the 'big house', the farm and outbuildings and twenty-six tenant holdings, cottages, each with five or seven acres of land. The River Geisthen, a tributary of that fine salmon river the Moy, skirted the confines of the estate in a fine big loop. By the river, less than a mile from the house, stood the remains of the Franciscan church of St Aidan, with a bee-hive cell nearby which, it was said, was once occupied by the saint. A body of Franciscan monks built the church, and for several centuries lived there among green meadows, the pleasant river flowing beside them. The present Killeaden farm buildings were their farm. The house at that time was probably

Killedan and its trees.

a small affair for a steward. Then sad days came, Cromwell stalked the land, the monks were swept away and a branch of the Knox family was given possession. The place remained in their hands until nearly two hundred years ago, when old Patrick Taaffe, a tall, devil-may-care sportsman, took over the place and improved it. His son, Frank Taaffe, kept hounds and both of them set more store by their horses and hounds and their cattle than they did by the grace of a home. Their horsemanship and carefree doings are still remembered in the countryside. It is said that Frank Taaffe 'walks' on Moonlight nights.

Anthony Raftery, the blind Irish-speaking poet and author was born at Ardroy estate, when it belonged to the Taaffes.

(Melrose, A., *Matron of Guy's*. London, 1956.)

MacManus's view of Raftery has a middle-class ring to it. Little did she know that Killedan would be remembered primarily because Raftery was born in the area. It is said that he was the son of a weaver from Co. Sligo. Illiterate, and blinded by smallpox in childhood, he was helped by his father's employer, Frank Taaffe, for whom he was a household entertainer, until they fell out, allegedly because he killed a favourite horse in an accident. The story is that he had gone to Kiltamagh on Taaffe's white horse to purchase drink, but the

Killeden Abbey.

horse fell into a stream and was killed. As a result, Raftery was banished from the area. So he became a wandering poet in south Galway. Often destitute, his life was free from normal constraints. According to a poetic rival he went with a woman called Siobhán, and they had two illegitimate children. The boy joined a circus, while the girl became a famous drunk. Douglas Hyde celebrated the life of the poet in his volume *Songs Ascribed to Raftery*. Raftery belonged to the hidden Ireland, the Ireland of the poor and the dispossessed. But his life was not without activity and wonder. He wrote many admirable poems and this simple and touching poem is well remembered. It has been translated from Irish:

> I am Raftery the poet,
> Full of hope and love,
> With eyes that have no light,
> With gentleness that has no misery.
> Going west upon my pilgrimage
> Guided by the light of my heart,
> Feeble and tired
> To the end of the road.

Behold me now,
And my face to a wall,
A playing music,
Unto empty pockets.

In 1900, Lady Gregory, Douglas Hyde and Edward Martyn erected a commemorative slab over his grave. He influenced the literary revival and his famous song 'Anois Teacht an Earraigh' is still sung in all Mayo schools.

Regretfully, we leave Killedan and journey to Kiltamagh. Reaching back in time we discover that Maghach was a Bronze Age chieftain. Returning from battle, he sought refuge on the wooded slopes of Sliabh Cairn, close to the town. He had fought and been wounded at the famous Battle of Moytura. After his death he was buried on the mountain, and that is the origin of the town Coillte Maghach the Woods of Maghach.

If you look up the boxer Gene Tunney's family records, you will find Gene Tunney's birth certificate, which lists his father as John J. Tunney, a thirty-seven-year-old stevedore who was born in Ireland. His mother was Mary Jean Lydon Tunney, a thirty-year-old housewife who was born in Ireland. Gene Tunney was listed as James Joseph Tunney, born 25 May 1897; and his parents' address was listed as 414 West 52nd Street, Borough of Manhattan. If they had been a little clearer, the records would have told us that Gene's father left Kiltamagh for the United States at the age of nineteen, and some years later his mother left Kiltamagh, also bound for the land of opportunity, where she met and married John Tunney. Gene was the heavyweight boxing champion from 1926 to 1928 and defeated Jack Dempsey twice: first, in 1926 and then again in 1927. Tunney's successful title defence against Dempsey is one of the most famous bouts in boxing history and is known as 'the Long Count Fight'. Tunney retired undefeated as a heavyweight after his victory over Tom Heeney in 1928. He died at the age of eighty-one and was both a film star and a successful businessman.

Kiltamagh is today a brightly painted town, with its own museum. The number of people who emigrated from Kiltamagh is higher than in most parts of Mayo. Their descendants are spread out all over the English-speaking world. We return to Bohola and take the road to Castlebar. We take a diversion and visit Turlough House.

Turlough

You slip quietly off the main road and turn right into Turlough. It is a quiet place and tranquil in its appearance. The land is rich and wooded. A small river runs by. It is a reedy river and sometimes it floods. Thus the name Turlough is derived from the river and the small plain which floods in the winter time. Perched on a hill to the right stands a dainty round tower and an elegant church is built snugly against it. The present building suggests to some that it belongs to the ninth or tenth century. The round tower is perfect in shape and carries a conical cap. Above the entrance to one of the doors stands a stark and beautiful depiction of the Crucifixion, filled with intense pity and sadness.

Close by are several raths set on high hills, commanding views of the countryside. They were enclosures protected at night by gates, when the animals were gathered in and sheltered from wolves. Several fulachta fia have been discovered in the area. These were cooking places built by the Bronze Age people. They consisted of a pit full of water, which was usually lined with timber or flat stones. Cooking was done by heating stones on a fire and then placing the hot stones in the pit. This boiled the water. Large chunks of meat would be placed in the fulacht fia to cook. Fulachta fia were still used well into the Iron Age. They survive in Ireland, Scotland, Wales and the Isle of Man, as low horseshoe-shaped mounds of charcoal-enriched soil and stones shattered by heat, with a slight hollow at its centre showing the position of the pit.

This gives us some idea of how long the area has been inhabited for. Good land will always attract planters. The De Burgos took up residence in Turlough as overlords in around 1450. Richard Bourke built a castle here. They remained in Turlough as overlords for many hundreds of years. Theobald Bourke joined in the Uprising and Civil War in 1641, and in 1655 was driven from his lands by the Cromwellian Commissioners.

The round tower at Turlough,
set upon a small drumlin.

The Cromwellian Commissioners transplanted John Fitzgerald from Gurteens, Co. Kilkenny, to Mayo. Several of the Fitzgeralds lost their estates in Kilkenny at the time. They came to Turlough and took possession of over 6,000 acres of land. They were a Catholic family who settled into their estates, married and set up family networks in Connaught. As with many other Mayo landowners, with the advent of the Penal Laws, Thomas Fitzgerald became a Protestant so as to hold on to his estate. Thomas built an eighteenth-century house, which is on the right as you enter the estate. It was built in 1722. It is a transition building, partly castle, partly house.

George Robert Fitzgerald was born in 1746, He was better known as 'the Fighting Fitzgerald'. He is reported to have fought in eleven duels by the time he reached the age of twenty-four. Although noted for eccentricity and toughness, even his opponents described him as a courtly and polite character.

In 1770, he married Miss Connolly, daughter of Thomas Connolly, who was an MP from Castletown in Co. Kildare, and received £30,000 by way of a dowry. After spending some time in Paris after the marriage, he returned to Dublin and lived in a mansion in Merrion Square, living a luxurious life in keeping with his position. Ten thousand pounds of the dowry was returned to his father, old George, in return for a deed promising him annual income. His father reneged on his promise, however. He, his lawyer friend, Seraglio, and his other son, Charles Lionel, conspired to deprive George Robert of his share of the estate. They employed Patrick Randall McDonnell to draw up long-term leases at low rents to some local tenants.

Old George was imprisoned for some time, during which George Robert took control of the estate. He improved the estate by planting trees and cultivating crops. George Robert brought a large number of linen workers from Ulster to Turlough in around 1870 so as to develop the linen industry. He gathered a body of volunteers called 'The Turlough Corps', who helped him in his quarrels. This colonisation resulted in the eviction of many Catholic families from the area.

Fitzgerald exercised his authority as a magistrate and a grand juror. He criticised the most powerful landlords in the area, the Brownes of Westport, the Binghams of Castlebar, and the Cuffes of Ballinrobe. His brother Charles Lionel and his father filed an indictment against him and he was sentenced to three years in jail. He escaped within the day, however, and captured his father, whom he held captive in a cave at Rockfield for fifteen months.

George Robert was executed because of an incident during which Brecknock, Fitzgerald's lawyer, and his fiancée were kidnapped and imprisoned at Glass Island in Lough Conn. The rescue of the lady fuelled the bitterness between George Robert and Patrick Randall McDonnell. Fitzgerald had McDonnell and two of his bodyguards, Hipson and Gallagher, arrested and held at Turlough House from where they were to be taken to Castlebar jail.

The next day, they tried to escape, which resulted in two of Fitzgerald's men shooting at them. Fitzgerald, Brecknock and Fulton were charged with murder, while Craig escaped with a life sentence for testifying against Fitzgerald. The County Sheriff, Mr Denis Browne, who was in charge of the trial, had long been an enemy of the Fitzgeralds. Brecknock, Fulton and Fitzgerald were sentenced to death by hanging. Two hours after their conviction Brecknock and Fulton were transported from the jail, then at the junction of Castle Street and Ellison Street, by cart to the new jail, the Bridewell, then under construction at The Mall, where they were hanged. An hour later Fitzgerald walked to the gallows and was hanged.

A new house, with the profile of a French chateau, was built in 1886 by T.N. Deane. The Fitzgeralds abandoned their Georgian house and set the new house upon a hill.

The plan of the new house is traditional, apart from the principal staircase, ingeniously contrived to pass over the front door so that its half-landing is a glazed Venetian loggia. The façade is symmetrical, with a high pitched roof and dormers, conveniently extended to a service wing and a lower stable block. The house was eventually sold to the Mayo County Council and became a national folk museum. The new buildings, covered with light grey granite and carrying great windows at the western end, almost float on the landscape.

We return to Castlebar, where our journey began. There have been many roads taken, but there are other roads which have not been taken. Small roads criss-cross the county, particularly in the triangle formed by Castlebar, Westport and Newport. I did not take the sea voyage between the uncountable islands of Clew Bay, some still inhabited. Neither have I taken the hill walks, which become more and more popular for this is a mountainous county to the west. There is so much more to tell, for Mayo is teeming with plenty. But for the moment the rest is silent.